Sex, Love and Abuse

Sex, Love and Abuse

Discourses on Domestic Violence and Sexual Assault

Sharon Hayes

Associate Professor, Queensland University of Technology, Australia

First published 2014 by
PALGRAVE MACMILLAN

Palgrave Macmillan in the UK is an imprint of Macmillan Publishers Limited,
registered in England, company number 785998, of Houndmills, Basingstoke,
Hampshire RG21 6XS.

Palgrave Macmillan in the US is a division of St Martin's Press LLC,
175 Fifth Avenue, New York, NY 10010.

Palgrave Macmillan is the global academic imprint of the above companies
and has companies and representatives throughout the world.

Palgrave® and Macmillan® are registered trademarks in the United States,
the United Kingdom, Europe and other countries.

ISBN 978–1–137–00880–0

This book is printed on paper suitable for recycling and made from fully
managed and sustained forest sources. Logging, pulping and manufacturing
processes are expected to conform to the environmental regulations of the
country of origin.

A catalogue record for this book is available from the British Library.

A catalog record for this book is available from the Library of Congress.

Transferred to Digital Printing in 2015

Contents

Foreword

Sex, Love and Abuse is a provocative book. While some may be shocked to read about fantasies of the zipless fuck, discussions about recreational sex and the candid frankness of the author, many who read its pages will be drawn into a skilfully crafted narrative interwoven with insightful reflection and analysis.

The book explains why men are wistful for masculinity and women wistful for romance, why the nexus between sex, love and abuse is such a powerful and enduring one. It also explores the heterosexualizing of girls' bodies and how those who do not fit the ideal are pathologized, unrequited, loathed or vulnerable to exploitation and abuse. According to the author, Sharon Hayes, most of us are inflicted by "brain spaghetti" when it comes to thinking our way through sex, love and romance. Why wouldn't we be, given the saturation of Disney Princesses consumed by most females during childhood. So much of contemporary and not so contemporary cinema and fairy tales reinforce this nexus, by promoting the myth that romantic love is always tragic, painful if not brutal or abusive. The link between romance, sacrifice and tragedy is epitomized by the heroine of *Twilight* – who literally has to be engulfed by her bloodsucking vampire lover to be saved from a pack of encroaching werewolves. The proliferation of pornography linking desire, subjugation and violence is another troubling aspect of the nexus between, sex, love and abuse.

The entrapment of romance and the power effects of love are themes interwoven into the analysis. Love is transformative and all-consuming. So much so, that sometimes it can transform into a dominating possessiveness where women especially may feel trapped and unable to leave abusive relationships. Many do not understand why. Sharon Hayes does. These are women caught in a dark romance because if they leave, they think they will lose their identity and status in the social world. They are blinded by the ideology of romance and think they will become nothing in a heteronormative world where women are measured and defined by their male partner.

The book also explains why so much of the discourse that we consume and take for granted is heteronormative – based on the assumption that excludes same-sex romance, sex and love. But even here Sharon Hayes points out that among othered sexualities, the nexus between sex, love and abuse can sometimes reign. The chapter on female sexual predators will no doubt shock many, as most assume that women are victims of sex offenders and not sexual predators. While this book challenges the essentialisms of feminism, it makes a significant contribution to the reconfiguration of feminist analysis that does not succumb to faith in false universalisms, that some-how all women are non-violent and all men violent, that all queer relationships are harmonious and non-queer abusive. Nothing is this simple. The book struggles against the ideologies of feminist backlash that have become so popular in the twenty-first century.

I found the argument and tone of this book tantalizing. It was such a compelling read it was hard to put down, regardless of how much I squirmed at times about the sentiments and arguments proffered. I eventually found relief in the last page of the book – that's it not a book about women and men whose relationships stand outside the parameters of those modelled on sex, love and abuse. I commend it to a wide range of readers, students and scholars across the social sciences, and hope you enjoy reading *Sex, Love and Abuse* as much as I did.

Professor Kerry Carrington
Head of School of Justice, Faculty of Law,
Queensland University of Technology
January 2014

Acknowledgements

Special thanks must go to my partner and daughter, both of whom provided input for this book, not to mention succour when I most needed it. I am very grateful for their patience. I also owe a huge debt to Samantha Jeffries, who has been discussing romantic love and domestic violence with me for many years. The seeds for many of the arguments in this book were planted in those discussions. Much also grew out of collaborations with Matthew Ball, Belinda Carpenter and Erin O'Brien, for which I am thankful. Jess Rodgers, who provided research assistance, was a tremendous help, as was Stephanie Jones, whose own research led to many fruitful discussions. Julia Willan and Harriet Barker from Palgrave showed incredible patience and support during the writing and publication processes. I am deeply indebted to Kerry Carrington for writing the Foreword and for providing ongoing encouragement and support for my research and writing. Finally, thanks must go to the Faculty of Law and the Centre for Crime and Justice at Queensland University of Technology for providing financial assistance at various points during this project.

1
Introduction

Love and sex are moral issues. Together, they probably contribute more drama and more joy to our lives than any other human pursuit. Love and sex feed into and underpin many of our relationships, though sometimes quite disparately. They may be mutually exclusive: the love of a parent for a child is commonly nurturing and sexless; sexual encounters or relationships may be loveless. And yet love and sex are mutually reinforcing. Adult intimate relationships in Western society often are underpinned by love, and yet, like sexual relationships based purely on physical desire, romantic love relationships may be sustained chastely. One only need view a few films or television programmes depicting human relationships to perceive the vast variety of ideologies surrounding the two concepts, and how precarious is our human understanding of how love and sex work – so much so, that we often feel we "get it wrong", that we can't understand how we keep making bad choices. Both traditional and contemporary discourses around love and sex tend to be contradictory or dissonant, at least some of the time, leading to distortions that may or may not be recognized as such. This book is an exploration of the morality of love and sex, and how distortions of these sometimes develop into abuse. I argue that there are strong similarities between different kinds of abusive relationships, and that these similarities arise out of the common narratives surrounding romantic love and the logic of intimate relationships.

Background

Recently, I was having dinner with some colleagues, one of whom had just read a chapter from a previous book I had published, and

1

I asked her what she thought. After the usual compliments, she cornered me with a question. Much of my work comes from philosophy, particularly moral philosophy – the study of morality and ethics – mingled with post-structuralist thinking, which aims, crudely, to deconstruct social and political phenomena as a way of challenging current norms and accepted wisdom. She remarked that, while the chapter was interesting and engaging, what exactly could it contribute to criminology? She then asked, more particularly, "What can you, as a philosopher, offer me as a criminologist?" I was gobsmacked by this question as, like most philosophers, I took the value of my work to be self-evident. It was at this point I experienced an epiphany of sorts. So some criminologists don't get me? That explains a lot!

At the time I think I mumbled some lame response, which was properly ignored (or should I say, smilingly tolerated and then silently dismissed) by my colleague, but the exchange proved to be one of the most important conversations of my career. Indeed, it was the start of a journey of sustained interrogation into my research, motivation and purpose that has culminated in the delivery of this book.

My thinking began quite fruitfully in the examination of just what is social science in general, and criminology in particular. Having worked in a multidisciplinary tertiary environment for many years, I had a fairly sophisticated understanding of the overall sociological imagination and the criminological project. My understanding was underpinned by formal and informal training in social science research methods and the conduct of qualitative projects in the field, and prior to my epiphany I had envisaged my contribution to be grounded in the philosophical analysis of what I saw as otherwise quite sterile research findings. Interviews with research participants were analysed through the lens of ancient and modern wisdom, social phenomena made sense of through the deconstruction of social discourses observed in the research process. I saw what I had to offer as a unique insight into social phenomena gained through the study of more than two millennia of philosophical wisdom and inquiry. Philosophy questions, it always questions, and this is the contribution I aimed to make. Philosophical inquiry also has political potential. As Stuart Hall famously notes, the study of society provides a starting point for observing and appreciating culture, while a philosophical perspective "gives intellectual expression to the possibility of something better" (Hall, cited in Williams 2012).

My first epiphany was confirmed fairly swiftly in another academic context – that of a French philosophers' reading group. As a multi-disciplinary but collegial school, we had decided to form a series of reading groups aimed at introducing our various "disciplines" and backgrounds to each other. The first text read by this group was Foucault's *Discipline and Punish*, a seminal work in penology, as well as an all-round good read. As a pre-eminent philosopher, Foucault has been widely read, cited and criticized over the past several decades, and while I do not place myself on level with such greatness ("Saint Foucault!"), I dared to hope that at least some of my work might address such issues as punishment and crime in a similarly thought-ful and provocative manner. So I was again taken aback when one of my colleagues suggested that, rather than profound philosophical insight, what Foucault offered us was really just observation, plain and simple. I walked away with much to think about.

This book examines the nexus between sex, love and abuse. In doing so, it also attempts to answer the question of what phi-losophy can offer to criminology. Tentatively and provocatively, my conclusion has been that it is not what value philosophy can add to criminology, but rather, what good criminology can be without attaching itself to some decent and hardworking philosophizing. This book aims to turn the tables, so to speak, by interrogating the crim-inological project from a philosopher's perspective. I do not claim to speak for philosophers as a group, by any means. There are many strands of philosophy, some of which completely contradict or refuse to speak to one another. The overarching aim of philosophy in gen-eral is clearer, however. Socrates argued that the unexamined life is not worth living. He initiated long discussions about the nature of human existence, including love, beauty and justice, among other ideals. Foucault was more interested in examining the social con-structions of civil society and how these governed individual and social identities. Both philosophers challenge us to explore the com-mon and the obvious with a view to uncovering the uncommon and exceptional. Observation certainly plays a part in this project, but observation is really only the very crude basis upon which inquiry can begin. It is inquiry that is the true purpose of philosophy, but not as an end in itself. Rather, inquiry is the instrument for uncovering the uncommon and exceptional, for exposing the nuances and complexities of humankind and the world in which we live. In this sense, it almost always has political potential because it uncovers similarities and differences pertaining to how we live together in society and the world.

"But what does it *do*?" my learned colleague pressed. "Why not just use the research that's already been done to explain, or do more research to uncover what hasn't yet been uncovered?" By research, of course, she meant empirical research. The question then, is: what good does inquiry do when we are trying to understand and do something about crime and criminality? To begin my answer, I turn first to a quote, not from a traditional philosopher, but from a respected writer of literature. Literature and philosophy overlap in many ways. One of those ways is through the use of poetic language to convey new and deeper meaning regarding some phenomenon. Another is through contemplation and reflection on observation.

In *Couples* (1968: Chapter 2), John Updike offers us the following insight into why someone might be blind to adultery:

> It is not difficult to deceive the first time, for the deceived possesses no antibodies; unvaccinated by suspicion, she overlooks lateness, accepts absurd excuses, permits the flimsiest patchings to repair great rents in the quotidian.

He could just as readily have said, "It's easy to deceive the inexperienced." Or even "Live and learn." But these seem sterile and crude in comparison. Updike uses literary language to paint a picture of deceit that brings home to us just how deeply flawed is the judgement of the vulnerable person. The deceived does not merely make excuses for her lover, she "permits the flimsiest patchings". She does not just overlook obvious lies, but "great rents in the quotidian". He provides us with images of a torn sheet or sail, an ordinary, everyday object (meant to serve us or comfort us) with great rips and tears through it. *That* is what deceit feels like to the uninitiated. The fabric of the relationship has been deliberately torn to pieces and yet she patches them up again and again in her naiveté, believing them to be caused by the wind and rain. The fact that she is "unvaccinated by deceit" delivers us imagery that depicts deceit as a disease to which we are vulnerable if we lack the requisite antibodies. This imagery lends us the perspective of the vulnerable, allows us to empathize with her. Turning a blind eye to adultery isn't so ridiculous when seen through her eyes. We feel compassion and understanding; indeed, we feel her pain.

It is because we are moved that we understand and gain insight into her naiveté. Updike has put us in her shoes. In our minds we become part of the tragedy and in this way acknowledge the complexity of life. Marcel Proust observed that "much literature and drama would conceivably have proved entirely unengaging, would have said nothing to us, had we first encountered its subject matter over breakfast in the form of a news-in-brief" (cited in de Botton 1998: 38). This observation cleverly unmasks the need for literary insight to broaden our understanding. Imagine opening the newspaper over a cup of tea and reading the small side headline "Woman shoots husband after years of violence. Details page 4." How unremarkable such headlines seem these days. We shake our head in disbelief; "Why didn't she just leave him?" we ask. Turning to page 4, we find a small square of words explaining the "details":

A woman from Capalaba has been found guilty of grievous bodily harm after shooting her husband of nine years around 9pm last night. Neighbours called police, who arrested the mother of two while paramedics attended the injured man, who was taken to Royal Brisbane Hospital for treatment. The woman, who pleaded guilty, said she was reacting to years of beatings by the husband. Justice Paragon handed down a suspended sentence.

None of this information tells us why she stayed in an abusive relationship, what the actual relationship was like for the woman and their children. How does someone become involved in such a relationship? What kind of society manages to perpetuate abuse in relationships? What purpose, if any, does abuse serve? *Why* didn't she just leave? These are questions left untouched by news stories – and for the most part, also by criminological research. Empirical research tells us that around one-third of relationships are abusive, that the vast majority of victims are women and perpetrators men (Renzetti 1992; Ristock 2002; Ball and Hayes 2011). Surveys of, and interviews with, women conducted in empirical research reveal the spectrum of abuses perpetrated on women, ranging from violent and physical, to emotional and financial. Theoretical research has taught us about the cycle of violence and psychological research about the perpetrators' need for control, their typically dysfunctional childhood relationships and victims' tendencies to co-dependency (Walker 1979). But none of this touches us or lends us insight so much as Stephen King's novel *Rose Madder,* or George Cukor's 1944 film, *Gaslight.* In *Gaslight,* Ingrid Bergman brilliantly portrays just how an intelligent and educated woman can easily succumb to the kinds of emotionally abusive tactics required to make her doubt her sanity. In *Rose Madder,* the heroine initially manages to escape many years of physical abuse, but her husband's relentless pursuit of her vividly exposes the intense fear and danger she had endured in the relationship, the hopeless resignation to daily pain and psychological torture. Even when women share their stories of abuse, either in the popular media, as memoirs, or in qualitative research studies, we may feel empathic to a degree, but we still find it difficult to understand the deeper meanings and personal impacts of the abusive relationship that kept the woman from leaving.

This book seeks to fill this gap by exploring the social and cultural milieu that allows abuse to flourish. It gratefully acknowledges the work of feminists, psychologists and criminologists in expanding our understanding of intimate partner abuse, but takes this understanding one step further by examining the governance of individuals and relationships through public discourses of love and sex. It addresses the questions of why there is "good" and "bad" love, "good" and "bad" sex, and why intimate relationships can be harmful. The book begins by exploring the contradictions inherent in Western attitudes towards love, sex and harm, and the tensions underlying the heteronormative imperative. It identifies constructions of romantic love and the erotic and how these are tied to harm and morality in intimate relationships. It unpacks and challenges the discourses surrounding current understandings of love, sex and abuse, and proceeds to explore some examples of harmful intimate relationships, specifically around intimate relationships between adults, and sexual relationships between generations.

To date, little scholarly research has been done from this perspective. While there are many feminist, criminological and psychological works on both intimate partner abuse and child sexual abuse, there is very little outside these dominant theoretical perspectives. Most of those that do challenge this normative framework do so from within an Lesbian, Gay, Bisexual, Transgender (LGBT) perspective, and are therefore fairly specifically focused on those groups. This book seeks to confront and interrogate the dominant paradigms and ask new questions such as whether it is possible for an individual to legitimately choose to stay in an abusive relationship without being pathologized, whether a woman can cause harm without being masculinized, why women who harm young children are not necessarily aberrations, and whether it is conceivable that a legally underage adolescent might consent to intimacy with an older partner – and what that means for dominant theories about harm, as well as current legislation surrounding it.

This book does not seek to construct a new theory about love, harm and intimacy. Rather, it seeks to destabilize essentialist understandings of these phenomena with a view to identifying the subtle and complex nature of relationships, such that they often defy easy explanation and categorization. It draws upon my previous theoretical work (Hayes and Carpenter 2012; Hayes et al. 2012; Hayes and Carpenter 2013), which also explores the morality of sex, but more specifically in relation to crimes such as prostitution, pornography, incest and sex trafficking. In the current book, I extend the moral and theoretical understandings of that work by focusing on theories, public discourses and moral ideals connecting romantic love, intimacy and harm. It is hoped this philosophical analysis lends a richer and more resonant impression of abuse in relationships and how such abuse is fostered.

Methodological considerations

In the service of these goals, I employ a range of explanatory and illustrative tools including auto-ethnography, hypothetical vignettes, case studies and discourse analysis. The use of hypotheticals in philosophy has a long tradition but it has also been used in social science, and even in survey design in criminology. In the latter context, vignettes provide a powerful quasi-experimental design which allows researchers to compare responses across randomly assigned characteristics, embedded in scenarios that remain constant across participants (Rossie and Nock 1982). In particular, this type of design has been previously used in criminological studies of public attitudes towards sentencing as well as perceptions of hate crimes (e.g. Rossie and Nock 1982; Lyons 2008). Since this book is not based on survey research, I use vignettes in the philosophical tradition, to create hypothetical scenarios or stories that reflect the particular ideas and discourses being discussed. These vignettes draw on real life stories, in order to more accurately reflect current understandings of the issues based on lived experiences, but remain essentially hypothetical for obvious ethical reasons – except where such stories are reported in public arenas such as published books and memoirs. It is hoped that the reader will thereby be able to imagine more profoundly the nature of abuse from the inside.

I also use auto-ethnography as an analytical tool to illustrate my arguments. Auto-ethnography explores the author's personal experiences and connects them to broader social, cultural and political discourses. It focuses on one's subjective experience and is therefore self-reflective and reflexive in its approach. It is evocative in that it does not seek to develop theoretical understandings of social and cultural phenomena; rather, it focuses "on narrative presentations that open up conversations and evoke emotional responses" (Ellingson and Ellis 2008: 445). The use of personal narrative in this book will provide space for developing conversations around romantic love, sex and sexuality, which help to explore it from within, rather than from an observer's perspective. Auto-ethnography is most often used in performance studies (e.g. Denzin 1997), cultural studies and education (e.g. Sambrook et al. 2008). Although it is not considered "mainstream", examples abound in scholarly journals (e.g. *Qualitative Inquiry, Journal of Contemporary Ethnography*) and books (e.g. Morrish and Sauntson 2007). It is narrative inquiry rather than autobiography because it draws on ahistorical moments and experiences as examples for analysis of the relevant discourses.

Discourse analysis is undertaken in the tradition of Foucault; that is, by examining the social, political, literary and scholarly dialogues surrounding love, sex and abuse, in order to identify power dynamics, strategies of governance and moments of resistance of the players involved. It is not a "critical discourse analysis" of the kind employed by scholars of linguistics or social science. It does not seek to enumerate the prevalence of particular phrases and ideas. Rather, it seeks to draw upon examples of the cultural context to expand our understanding of the issues and to challenge accepted wisdom.

As mentioned above, the current research is also transdisciplinary. It has been argued that transdisciplinarity can be a "transformative experience" in scholarly research, both for its explanatory and political potential (Moran 2002). Claxton (1997: 71) argues that knowledge should be viewed as a set of maps, each of which provides a particular kind of information and which, when juxtaposed, provides a deeper understanding and complexity that can ultimately guide us towards a better understanding. As Elshof (2003) remarks, transdisciplinarity organizes knowledge in new ways, across sectors and disciplines, thereby allowing scientific and social knowledge to complement and challenge each other for political change (Elshof 2003: 167).

The use of case studies is fairly uncontroversial, having been a commonly used methodology in social science in recent times. The case studies used in this book, however, were chosen as "methodological release points" (McClelland and Fine 2008: 243):

> that is, data analysis that allows us to expand out methodological imaginations beyond oversimplified "telling it like it is" accounts and thus open up our interpretations in ways that "help us think" through how we might take a young women's words at face value and analyse what she may or may not necessarily be able to willingly see, feel, speak, know or reveal.
>
> (Renold and Ringrose 2011: 395)

It is hoped that this mixed methodological approach allows for a more thorough and complex analysis of the issues at hand, with a view to uncovering possible explanations for the unanswered questions outlined above, concerning the nexus between sex, love and abuse.

Structure

While the book as a whole aims to provide a set of interconnected and cross-referential arguments in a way that flows naturally from beginning to end, each chapter may be read as a stand-alone piece of work with its own research questions, analysis and discussion. The following brief outlines of the chapters allow the reader who is short of time to immediately direct their attention to topics of interest.

Chapter 2 provides a critical analysis of discourses of romantic love and how they relate to sex and relationships. It explores the nature of romance, how men and women in our society are taught to think about it, and the contradictions arising out of clashes between differing discourses. It draws on examples from popular culture to illustrate this.

Chapter 3 explores how media depictions of femininity and romantic love impact culture and influence the way we think about gender, bodies and relationships. It draws on examples from the Disney Princesses franchise to discuss how femininity is constructed in young girls, and what impact this has on men's and women's expectations of love and relationships and their physical manifestations.

Chapter 4 draws on and further expands the analysis of femininity in popular culture in Chapter 3 to discuss how society valorizes victimhood and the tragedy of romantic love and how this provides at least some explanation for why women and girls enter into and stay in abusive relationships. It analyses narratives from online discussion forums to illustrate this.

Chapter 5 explores the geography and temporality of sex and how our perceptions of sex and sexuality have developed over time. It draws on moments from history to illustrate how discourses have changed and what that means for contemporary sexuality. It also challenges intrinsic notions of moral harm frequently associated with sex and crime via a critical interrogation of dominant discourses surrounding public and private spaces, and Western and non-Western spaces.

Chapter 6 looks at contemporary constructions of masculinity and femininity and how they relate to the sexual assault of women. It explores and unpacks a disturbing trend towards misogyny, and argues that it is part of a larger backlash against feminism that is dogging Western nations as a whole. It compares this trend to historical analyses by feminists such as Faludi (1991), who documented an earlier backlash against feminism and girl-power in the 1990s, characterized by a return to hegemonic masculine values and behaviours, especially among the working class. It explores why "the bro code" is not necessarily confined to the working class, and how it contributes towards everyday sexism against women.

The concept of the sexual predator is explored in Chapter 7, with a particular focus on how predation is tied to gendered subjectivities and love distortion. Contemporary discourses suggest that women cannot be predators and men cannot be victims. The aim of this chapter is to challenge dominant ideas about gender and sexual predation by exploring the ways in which we construct sex offenders, and specifically female sex offenders. While male sex offenders are always cast as predators, female sex offenders are often made out to be victims, given the vulnerable role. This, I argue, is consistent with the pervasiveness and insidiousness of sexism in our society, because it infantilizes women and constrains their subjectivity.

Chapter 8 aims to provide a summary of the arguments made in the preceding chapters, and attempts to draw the threads of those arguments together in order to make sense of the nexus of sex, love and abuse. It identifies two main issues: first, how do we reconcile the Disney/*Twilight* version of romance and enchantment with the expectation of sexual freedom? Second, and probably more importantly, it asks how we might address the production of sexism and misogyny that appear to underlie discourses of abuse in our society, and how we might best proceed in politicizing the social as a way of addressing domestic violence and sexual assault.

2
Enchantment and Romance

Introduction

My sister describes the state of something being a psychological or personal "issue" for someone – a trauma, compulsion, phobia, or obsession, for example – as "having brain spaghetti". For example, apparently she has spaghetti about me pinning her down as a child and tickling her until she screamed for mercy. She knows this because when her spouse tried to do the same, the experience she had as a child came flooding back as a complex tangle of fears, feelings and mental images. Notwithstanding the trauma inflicted on a sibling in my youth, the spaghetti metaphor is a simple but useful tool for explaining how complex our experiences are, and I bring it up here because I believe a lot of people have spaghetti about love.

In this chapter I explore the idea of love, particularly romantic love, and how people might come to have spaghetti about it. I also expand my earlier claim that love is a moral issue by examining the discourses surrounding it. In Western society, we grow up on a diet of popular discourses about relationships and what they mean. Many of these discourses are gendered – where intimate relationships are concerned, for men the discourse is predominantly about sex, for women it is romantic love, although of course the division is not so black and white. Discourses about love and sex also tend to be predominantly heteronormative, which is to say, focused on hetero-sexual monogamous relationships and traditional masculinity and femininity. Nevertheless, as we shall see, sex and love are two issues over which spaghetti abounds, and the relationship between the two is probably one of the most complex with which people of all genders and sexualities in our society are faced. To that end, this chapter will examine some of the more enduring discourses characterizing romantic love and what they might mean for us.

Discourses of romantic love

The discourse of enchantment

In popular culture, romantic love is first and foremost a discourse of enchantment. Christina Perri, for example, sings about loving someone for a thousand years, and notions such as this abound in popular music, literature, film, and everyday parlance.

> I have died everyday waiting for you
> Darling don't be afraid I have loved you
> For a thousand years
> I'll love you for a thousand more[1]

Simplistically, we might think of Perri's words as a metaphor for the pain and yearning experienced while waiting for the "right person" to come along. When we meet "the one", we feel as if we have known them forever, and that finally, fate has brought us together. When we meet our destined partner, our soul mate, we become enchanted with each other and with love itself. "A Thousand Years" was made popular as part of the soundtrack for the *Twilight*[2] film series and echoes with excruciating precision the discourse played out between the two main characters, Bella and Edward. I will explore the *Twilight* series in more detail later in this chapter and in chapters 4 and 6. At this point, I want to focus on the song itself and how it beautifully depicts some of the most compelling contemporary discourses about romantic love. In doing so, I have no intention of demonizing love, or setting it up as a "straw man" responsible for all the ills in our society. Rather, I want to explore the richness of the concept and how deeply rooted it is within the psyche of many contemporary relationships.

Indeed, "A Thousand Years" resonates with me personally. Having been married and divorced, then through two unsuccessful relationships over the past 20-odd years, I was determined that I was better off without intimate relationships, happy to live peacefully with my almost-grown up daughter and enjoying the solitary contentment of having (for the most part) only myself to worry about. In fact, as a philosopher, a researcher and a feminist, I had analysed love and relationships to death, and come to the conclusion that women have been duped by romance for far too long. Nevertheless, one summer a couple of years ago I met someone who managed to do what I considered the impossible. I met my partner in November but we really didn't date until January. I didn't want a relationship and said so several times. Jaded feminist that I am, I let it pass as the usual infatuation, figuring it would dissipate quickly and I would have my solitude back. She persisted, however, and at the airport one evening on her way to New Zealand, she texted me the name of a song and asked me to look for it online. I was lying in bed playing on my iPad when I watched the music video of Christina Perri singing "A Thousand Years". Uncharacteristically, I burst into tears.

"Head over heels" might seem like a strange term, even if you are, liked most of us, used to hearing it in common parlance about love and romance. However, it describes perfectly the rush of feeling, the lightheaded, confused happiness and delight that come with realizing that someone you like and admire loves you *that* much. So much, in fact, that it trips you into the "fall" that becomes romantic love. Now, I have to admit the jaded feminist in me prevented me from crossing into the foolish infatuation, the "crushed" romantic so well depicted in literature and film. My research and philosophizing about love had taught me what a mature intimate relationship should look like. Thus I endured the puppy eyes and mushy endearments of my lover only up to a point. I still, however, willingly bought into the romance and at least some of its common accompaniments, including commitment and, in fact, have mellowed out considerably from jaded to hopeful, even contented. The question is, how does someone like myself, who has deconstructed all the discourses on romance, and understands in minute detail how distorted and harmful much of it is, come to be "in love"? Apparently, this is a question many feminists ask of themselves under similar circumstances.

In the introduction to her edited collection, *Jane Sexes it up: True Confessions of Feminist Desire* (Johnson 2002), Merri Lisa Johnson explores just that question. She bemoans the fact that, as a feminist, she knows that all the heteronormative hype of romance is problematic, but at the same time wants it anyway:

Growing up with feminism is like an eccentric aunt always reminding us how smart we are, how we can do anything, be anyone, the women of my generation hesitate to own up to the romantic binds we find ourselves in, the emotional entanglements that compromise our principles as we shuttle back and forth between *feminist* and *girlfriend, scholar* and *sex partner.*
                                                   (Johnson 2002: 14. Emphasis in original)

Johnson (2002: 15) goes on to argue that, if feminism is right, these obstacles signal "personal failures, individual shortcomings in the face of unlimited feminist opportunity". She then immediately confesses to trying to convince a man to marry her for four years! In a discussion of the film *Jerry Maguire*, where Tom Cruise's character, Jerry, begs his wife to come back with the famous line, "You complete me", Johnson (2002: 16) responds "Ohgodjesus [sic] – I could live on that for the rest of my life." Clearly we are talking about some very complex discourses here.

Johnson claims that "Gen X" is confused by these conflicting messages, but I believe that this is understated – baby boomers like myself and some of my colleagues and friends are also feeling it, as are Gen Y's. Indeed, Stevi Jackson was writing about this phenomenon as early as 1993 in her now famous paper "Even Sociologists Fall in Love" and it seems that since then little has changed for our generation. Indeed, it seems spaghetti abounds no matter which generation you belong to. To illustrate this point, I now turn back to the *Twilight* saga film series, which provides a wealth of examples.

Interestingly, as I noted above, the female lead in the series is named Bella. One can't help but make the automatic association between her character and that of Belle in Disney's *Beauty and the Beast*. Both characters are troublesome. Belle, the "Beauty" in the Disney film, is captured by a cranky beast who lives in a huge castle. Belle is the quintessential beautiful young ingénue who wins the beast over with her kind words and sweet manner. The facts that she has traded herself for the safety of her father and that the beast is abusive are downplayed, overtaken by the romantic storyline, where Belle eventually, through her sweetness and love, turns the beast into the perfect prince and they get married and live happily ever after.

The Bella of *Twilight*, on the other hand, willingly falls under the spell of a century old vampire, Edward Cullen, who still looks 17.

Theirs is a very traditional and chaste relationship, though there is much sexual tension arising from the traditional values underlying Edward's gentlemanly refusal to give into Bella's lust for him (Kokkola 2011). The first time they meet, he yearns to suck her blood, but forces himself to contain his desire because he and his "family" (a group of vampires the creation of which stems back to the "father", Carlisle Cullen) are "good" vampires who don't kill people, preferring to dine only on animal blood. His desire for her blood is mingled with passionate romantic desire and a sense of the destiny of their meeting, both of which he feels he must suppress because he is too powerful and too ethical. She falls for him anyway, and the first two films are spent arguing the "fors" and "againsts" of them having sex and a relationship. Apparently he is so strong that he fears crushing her in his embrace, but also fears for her getting involved with him, as the only result can be her eventual death and transformation into a vampire like himself. In spite of Bella begging Edward to kill and transform her, he remains resolute, at least until the third film, where they marry and he whisks her off to Brazil for a honeymoon from which she returns covered in bruises. Eventually, he is forced to kill her and make her a vampire in order to save her from some Italian vampire Nazis.

If you have not had the dubious luck to have seen these films, my short summary might cause you to wonder how on earth an otherwise sane 17-year-old girl could be so masochistic. And there lies the main similarity between the Bella and Belle. Where Disney's Belle transforms her beast through suffering and love, *Twilight's* Bella is herself transformed by her suffering and love. Historically, this transformative notion of love is deeply embedded in Western culture. Burns argues that "the notion of romantic love in its idealistic, redemptive and sensual version" has been around since the twelfth century, when French poets such as Chrétian de Troys wrote about romantic love as a "transformation of desire" (Besley 1994: 97; cited in Burns 2000)

> Historically, passionate romantic love has been imbued with the ability to challenge traditional structures and taboos, to survive obstacles (even death) and to be a symbol of freedom and redemption to the extent that obstacles become an integral part of the love trajectory.
>
> (Burns 2000: 482)

Bauman (2004), however, contends that the challenges of love inevitably lead to its demise; indeed, that love is always fatally transformed by its own achievement. Individuals who fall in love seek to fuse their duality into the "couple". Love seeks to care for, to protect and therefore to possess, but the possessed will always seek freedom, and this tension is what ultimately forms love's death wish. As Bauman (2004: Loc250) states, "Eros prompts a hand to be stretched toward the other – but hands that may caress may also clutch and squeeze," and goes on to name "possession, power, fusion, and disenchantment" as the Four Horsemen of the Apocalypse for love.

The key to its destruction, he claims, is love's desire for the other: "The protective net which love weaves caringly around its object enslaves its object. Love takes captive and puts the apprehended in custody; it makes an arrest, for the prisoner's protection" (Bauman 2004: Loc 281). Nevertheless, people continue willingly to believe that love's transformation is more like a "beautiful nightmare" – the sacrifice of the self, well worth the price. If sacrifice can transform the damaged and broken into something glorious and enduring, then sacrifice is a virtue, something to aspire to.

This is nowhere clearer than in *Beauty and the Beast*. Disney's Beast is ugly and mean, but Belle's willingness to sacrifice herself together with her ability to understand her Beast's true inner (kind and courageous) self, transforms him into a kind and handsome prince, the ultimate prize. *Twilight's* Edward, on the other hand, while potentially dangerous, is devastatingly handsome, which accords much more favourably to a Gen Y audience brought up in a society where appearances mean everything (Kokkola 2011). He is still a monster, but a good-looking one, and he also proves his worthiness by trying to protect Bella from her fate. How can she *not* fall for him and eventually convince him to proceed with the transformation that means they will be together forever?

One has to ruefully concede that *Twilight's* Bella *will* love her Edward for a thousand years (and more)! The eternity of vampirehood is a rather crude metaphor for the eternity of romantic love, which is meant to endure until death and even after. The message is clear – "true" romantic love is enduring and worth suffering for. Taylor (2012: 31) argues that this combination of "masochistic" relationship and Bella's "yearning for an undead subjectivity" is perceived as a "utopic site of possibility" for teens. This is bolstered by the perception that their love is also fated, written in the stars, orchestrated so that they have no say in it. In Chapter 4, I will explore distortions of love and the relationship between love and suffering. For now, the important point is that in popular culture individuals are regarded as helpless in the face of love – which is not necessarily a bad thing, in spite of its dubious perspicacity.

Indeed, the hand of fate may usefully be blamed for many happy relationships, given the chances of actually finding someone compatible with whom one can tolerably live in close quarters for possibly decades, let alone feel close enough to maintain love. Alain de Botton (1997: 75) discusses "the general difficulty of maintaining an appreciative relationship with anything or anyone that was always around". His discussion of Marcel Proust's *In Search of Lost Time* is instructive. Proust's narrator is besotted by Gilberte. He cannot stop thinking about her, his every waking moment is taken up with imagining what she is doing and wearing. Eventually, they become friends and his yearning is finally requited. She invites him to tea and he marvels in her beauty and grace. The more he sees of her, however, the more his interest wanes.

> ...after a quarter of an hour in her drawing room, it is the time before he knew her, before she was cutting him cake and showing him affection, that starts to grow chimerical and vague.... [This] suggests that having something physically present sets up far from ideal circumstances in which to notice it. Presence may in fact be the very element that encourages us to ignore or neglect it.
>
> (de Botton 1997: 177, 179)

de Botton cleverly understands and expresses just how fickle our desires can be, remarking conversely that, quite logically, "deprivation drives us into a process of appreciation" (de Botton 1997: 179). In other words, we always want that which seems out of reach. Familiarity breeds contempt, as the old adage goes. The role of romance is to seduce us into believing that we *can* sustain desire for longer than it takes for the ink to dry on the marriage certificate. Thus, romance serves the dual purpose of maintaining heteronormative institutions such as marriage and monogamy, while giving people hope that a long future with the chosen one won't turn into bored familiarity. Why else would people spend tens of thousands of dollars on elaborate weddings?

Eva Illouz (1997: 2) draws on this "connection between love and economy", arguing that "romantic love has become an intimate, indispensable part of the democratic ideal of affluence that has accompanied the emergence of the mass market, thereby offering a collective utopia cutting across and transcending social divisions". There are clear links between the economic function of marriage and the wedding ritual, which is a rite of passage throughout the developed world and is illustrated and depicted through popular culture – in film plots, for example, where lovers experience intense attraction to the point that they "are willing to endure separation in order to achieve union" (Wilding 2003: 373). The wedding marks the couple's commitment to an enduring future together, demonstrated by economic markers of consumption and extravagance deemed appropriate for only the most important of social occasions. Marriage thereby becomes one of the modes of cultural transmission and social organization through which society is reproduced (Rosenblatt 1966; Coppinger and Rosenblatt 1968).

Berlant (2011) claims that these consumer-driven institutions work as vehicles for the reproduction of culture and society. She remarks that marriage and weddings rely on and reinforce "the temporality of the workday, the debt cycle and consumer practice and fantasy" (Berlant 2007: 765). In particular, the fantasies of upward mobility, political and social equality, job security and "lively and durable intimacy", through which one "builds a life", are reproduced via "the processes and procedures involved historically in the administration of law and bodies". Romantic love, particularly the discourse of enchantment, governs bodies in particular ways for capitalist ends, reproducing the neo-liberal tendency to what Berlant (2011) calls "cruel optimism" – that is, the continued, mostly illusory hope for realization of the social-democratic promise of a life fulfilled.

But the economic imperative that impels lovers to plan weddings and honeymoons also has a darker side. According to Bauman, consumer culture treats love and relationships much like every other commodity – one shops for love much as one shops for a new outfit (Bauman 2003: 12). If it gives the expected satisfaction, then we keep it; if it's flawed, we take it back and find a new one. However, I think this fails to account for the enduring nature of the concepts of soul mate and spouse, both of which imply forever, and the expectation – the hope at least – that this one *will* be enduring. The wedding and honeymoon are symbolic of this intent to endure, and their playing out represents our enchantment with the chosen other and with love. The sheer amount of money spent on such things is at least partially meant to mark the ceremoniousness of the occasion where one agrees to give up once and for all one's freedom to love and desire any other. Nevertheless, we have to concede that Bauman is correct at least in claiming that the wished-for eternity of love often dissipates. In the following section, I consider the psychological discourses surrounding love and what it means to be in love.

Psychological discourses

The entry for Romantic Love in the *Encyclopedia of Social Psychology* (Aron et al. 2007) surveys several explanations for how love "works". The first emphasizes evolutionary anthropology, which suggests that romantic love "evolved to motivate individuals to select among potential mating partners" (Aron et al. 2007: 767). After the initial passionate period wanes and they have mated, they then settle into a calmer, more appropriate relationship for raising children. The habituation theory, on the other hand, supports de Botton's thesis that familiarity with the beloved results in romantic decline (Aron et al. 2007: 766). The authors claim, however, that romantic love does not necessarily always weaken. Apparently romance is enhanced when we experience exciting and challenging events together – both trauma and intense joy can bolster romantic feelings. Indeed,

> One study found that men who met an attractive woman when on a scary suspension bridge were more romantically attracted to her than were men who met the same woman on a safe bridge.
>
> (Aron et al. 2007: 765)

Thus, couples that "do challenging and novel activities together" are more likely to maintain the romance in their relationship (Aron et al. 2007: 766). However, these psychological explanations fail to account for the fact that, these days, people do not need to fall in love to procreate. The broadening of our sexual discourses to endorse recreational sex and sex outside of marriage and monogamy, not to mention common acceptance of individuals who choose to parent without a long-term partner, suggest that we don't need love to get sex and babies (Hayes et al. 2012). It also fails to account for the place of romantic love in non-heterosexual relationships.

Branden (2008: 47) argues that in order to understand love, we must first consider "aloneness – the universal condition of us all". He employs a developmental model based on the maturation of the self through separation and individuation to understand the need for romantic love. As young children, we develop our sense of self by separating from our carers and striving to develop an individual identity. But separation and individuation are not just childhood tasks. We are continually confronted by the need to re-establish our identities – when a romantic love relationship ends, when a long-term partner dies, when our children leave home, we are once again left to determine just who we really are without the context of the particular relationship in question.

> We can strive to avoid the fact of our ultimate aloneness; it continually confronts us. A romantic love relationship can nourish us; it can become a substitute for personal identity.
>
> (Branden 2008: 48)

In a society in which extended families are no longer the norm, and in which increased geographical movement makes even the concept of community less common, romantic love helps fill a gap, providing us with a way of identifying that denies or hides, for the time being at least, our ultimate aloneness. But even if it does serve a unique purpose for contemporary individuals, romantic love was not invented by Western industrial society – according to the literature, it has been around for millennia.

Aron et al. (2007: 765) claim that "romantic love has been found in every historical era and in every culture for which data are available". Notwithstanding the ambiguity of "available data" and the fact that none of the claims in their encyclopaedia entry are referenced, there does seem to be some consensus concerning the long history and cultural inclusivity of romantic love, although it is often noted that the connection of romantic love to marriage is far more recent (discussed below). Evidence can be found as far back as the Ancient Greeks, in the concepts of Eros, Agape and Platonic love (Soble 1989). Tales of Eros in Ancient Greek mythology talk of being shot through the eye with an arrow – love at first sight – where physical attraction to another is both piercing and tragic, has the ability to make one insane, and is something over which one has no control. Agape is love as an end in itself, love for someone that requires nothing in return, such as a parent's love for their child. Platonic love is the love felt between two people without the sexual attraction. From ancient times, through the dark and middle ages and right up until today, love has taken one form or another, sometimes romantic, sometimes altruistic, sometimes tragic, sometimes divine.

But it was only after the Enlightenment and Western industrialization that love became attached to marriage and families. In Ancient Greece, Socrates talks about Eros only in reference to what is felt by a man for a beautiful boy. In that context, families and marriage were completely removed from notions of romantic love (Soble 1989). Throughout most of history and across cultures, marriages were arranged by kin to combine property or as part of the exchange relations between male kin groups, for example, a man giving a sister in order to obtain a wife. Romantic love emerged in medieval Europe, but it was something that happened specifically outside marriage, often between troubadours and ladies. Sir Lancelot, for example, loved his best friend's wife, Guinevere. In fact, marriage and family remained completely unrelated to Eros until mid to late nineteenth century, while marriage as an institution remained completely heteronormative until the early twenty-first century (Coontz 2005).

How did romance, marriage and family become so intimately connected? While it is clear that we as a society are slowly diverging from the ideal of the heteronormative nuclear family, the fact still remains that young women – intelligent, educated young women – are lining up to spend fortunes on fairytale weddings and honeymoons, are taking their husbands' names, and treading the traditional path to family and domesticity (Ingraham 2008). I personally attended two weddings last year alone, one for a friend, another for my partner's niece. Both were magnificent affairs featuring many bridesmaids, plenty of beautiful flower arrangements, champagne, and the traditional long white dress and veil. One couple went to the Maldives afterward, the other on an extended tour of the USA and Mexico, including resorts such as Cancun. Both have settled into domesticity and are planning families. Clearly, normative values surrounding romance and the wedding are alive and supporting huge industries in fashion, beauty, catering and international travel.

In the scholarly literature there is a great deal of debate over whether romantic love is a cultural construct (e.g. Lystra 1989; Person 1991; Jankowiak and Fischer 1992; Illouz 1997; De Munck 1998; Wilding 2003). Person (1991: 383) for example, argues that "the best evidence that romantic love is not hardwired... but is a cultural construct is the fact that there are so many cultures in which it is virtually absent". However, Jankowiak and Fischer (1992: 149) argue to the contrary that romantic love is definitely not unique to the West; that indeed, it is "characteristic of many non-Euro cultures, for example, China". Nevertheless, whichever side you take, it does seem that romantic love takes on a very peculiar form in our Western society, and it is this cultural milieu that provides the context for this book. That peculiar form is characterized, as we have seen above, by "an intense attraction involving the idealization of the other within an erotic context... [which] carries with it the desire for intimacy and the pleasurable expectation of enduring for some unknown time into the future" (Wilding 2003: 373).

The geography of love is marked by the very public definition of love's expectations, along a trajectory where "going out together" morphs into being a "couple", which is inevitably followed by public displays of affection and commitment culminating in the wedding. These public displays assist in the constitution of identity and subjectivity and outline the expectations within which the couple experience their life together. It is "a closing off of emotional ambivalence... a movement away from contingency towards unity and towards an emotional paradise of reciprocity and certainty" (Wetherall 1995: 128). These expectations remain strong in spite of the high levels of divorce and infidelity in the West. Indeed, as I will discuss later in this section, infidelity and divorce form part of the narrative that paradoxically reinforces romantic love as grounding for intimate relationships. Wetherall (1995: 128) agrees that discourses of romance provide a trajectory of the life of the couple, which is experienced as a "form of relief from the search for meaning" so clearly lacking, as Berlant (2011) points out, from many peoples' lives.

> We move from the image of the couple (usually newly met) locked in a maelstrom of ambiguities, partial disclosures, interpretations and formulations of their relationship to the predictable ending of romance which stifles other interpretations and imposes its

authority over other accounts. In the end he loved her, that is the final story....

(Wetherall 1995: 128)

With the uncertainty of any particular marriage lasting, it does seem reasonable to think that two people who can say they love and cherish each other after decades of living together must have been destined for each other. It is common knowledge that at least half of marriages end in divorce, and yet we still believe in the idea of fate and lifelong romantic love. This discourse runs so deeply that even serial romances don't deter us or alter our thinking on the subject. On the contrary, the fact that some couples *do* live happily ever after seems to be enough to give us the hope necessary to sustain the discourse. B.F. Skinner (1953) famously conducted a scientific experiment that illustrates this point. He trained rats to press a lever to obtain food, then instead of feeding the rats each time they pressed the lever, he made them wait for one minute. He discovered that rewarding the rats with food intermittently (instead of each time they pressed the lever) made them press the lever more often, not less, as he had expected. Apparently the intermittent reinforcement is enough to keep the rat hooked. Poker machines work the same way.

The discourse of the loving marriage

Are we then simply like rats hooked on love through intermittent reinforcement? Or is there something more complex than mere Pavlovian psychology going on here? I suggest that romantic love remains so ubiquitous because the discourse of the loving marriage is deeply and insidiously ingrained in our collective psyches. Indeed, the myth of enduring marriage persists in spite of the evidence that the larger percentage of marriages end in divorce, that infidelity is a fact of life and that time and again our expectations of that institution are proven to be too high.

> ... the real fault in the situation lies in the ethos of modern marriage, with its insane ambitions and its insistence that one person can plausibly hope to embody the eternal sexual and emotional solution to another's every need.
>
> (De Botton 2012: 117)

Here, de Botton defends infidelity against what he sees as the insanity of the romance discourse. "Some people would never have fallen in love if they had never heard of love" (La Rochefoucauld, cited in de Botton 2006: 76), he quips, while also pointing out, as we have already discussed above, that current discourses of love and marriage are "kept alive by modern capitalism" through the nuclear family, which supports current market structures (de Botton 2006: 77).

A review of the relevant scholarly literature appears to support the argument that the "marriage for love discourses" are relatively recent (Cott 2000; Coontz 2005; Wood 2011). However, the neo-Marxist, economic rationalist argument seems a bit too neat. Nuclear families arose in the wake of increased wealth and opportunity. Generations no longer need to live together under one roof in order to survive financially; women are more independent and no longer need to marry to survive. Women and men have a choice of whether and who to marry. The ability to marry the person you desire and love was originally seen as liberating, and still is (Clulow 1993; Cott 2000; Chambers 2001). Indeed, we scoff at the person who marries for convenience, social status or money – in our society, the only truly ethical option is to marry for love. Although increased technology and vastly improved transportation means that people are moving around geographically more than ever before and global markets have opened up opportunities that appeal to young couples and families, it seems rather a stretch – too much like conspiracy theory – to suggest that capitalism by itself is responsible for the concept of the loving marriage.

Indeed, in an era where individuals are more independent than ever before, people are *choosing* to get married and have children, or to set up nuclear households outside marriage (Cott 2000). It is true that the current high-priced housing market in Australia, where I live, leans towards smaller families, but that is not necessarily a global trend. Housing in almost every other Western nation is cheaper than here in Australia, depending upon whether you are situated in intense urban or more suburban or rural locations. A more subtle explanation is therefore needed, perhaps a combination of economic necessity, market pressure, a characteristically modern Western desire for acceptance and validation, and the need to believe that there is something outside oneself and one's fragile human existence that survives us and leaves a legacy for future generations (Bauman 2004).

In spite of the enduring impact of religious influence in the Western world (Newport 2012), the psychological literature shows there is a clear gap in our perceptions of mortality and all that that means (Shaver and Mikulincer 2012). Newport (2012), *Gallup* Editor-in-Chief (of the famous *Gallup Polls*) reports that Americans at least, are still highly religious, but clearly even religions – at least those dominating the West – strongly support marriage for love, although the more fundamentalist of these are outspoken about their contempt for the concept of a "soul mate" (Keller and Keller 2013). Clearly, there remains a need for the romance discourse to make sense of our relationships. The need to believe in the romance discourse also compensates us for the fact that our liberal-democratic society has a definite tendency towards individualism, and yet, as human animals, we need to interact, not to isolate (Branden 2008). It also compensates for the fact that we, as individuals, aren't very good folk psychologists (Goldie 2007). In spite of feeling "as one" with a romantic partner, we likely know very little of their inner lives, let alone our own. People are notoriously irrational when it comes to most things and romantic love probably sits somewhere on the rationality scale between our self-image (which is always predicated on skewed perception) and what we know of others (which is always predicated on what they are willing to show us). Of necessity, we operate within "bounded rationality" in which decision-making is necessarily limited by how much information we have, how intelligent we are, and how much time we have or are willing to take in doing so (Simon 1972).

de Botton (2006: 15) argues that "every fall into love involves the triumph of hope over self-knowledge". At the same time as serial romance fails to hinder us in our quest for our soul mate, we also are not hindered by the fact that the person with whom we are currently in a relationship could easily be replaced by any number of people. Indeed, I would argue that this fact is most vehemently denied – we much prefer to believe that the end of a relationship or loss of a love simply means that we were mistaken in thinking we had found "the one"; so we must keep on searching until we do. We might also argue that love not only triumphs over self-knowledge, but also what appears before our very eyes. The loved one is always unique, different, idealized as the perfect match (de Botton 2006). As long as we can sustain that fiction, we stay "in love". As we will see in Chapter 4, even abuse can be obscured or accepted if we fail to understand the difference between appearances and actualities. The narcissistic partner, for example, initially comes across as attentive, will put you on a pedestal and idealize you, lulling you into a false sense of the security and enchantment of romantic love (Lowen 2004). Our lack of psychological knowledge or understanding of much human behaviour allows us to miss certain cues that should be "red flags" when the narcissist's façade starts to crack (Lowen 2004; Hayes and Jeffries 2013). Romantic love blinds us to flaws, at least initially, until we are comfortable enough to accept each other for who we are. When the "real" self differs too much from the idealized self, we may find ourselves making excuses until it becomes glaringly clear that love has turned into abuse.

Love is also associated with ownership and licence (Burns 2000; Wilding 2003; de Botton 2006). Although there are many more open and polyamorous relationships today than ever before, the popular heteronormative, *Twilight* version of romantic love implies possession. Thus, infidelity and absence without reason are seen as offences against the relationship. The degree to which we treat our beloved as property rather than with the respect and trust due to them as our equals, directly reflects the extent to which we have bought the heteronormative discourse of romantic love. I would argue that this applies equally to same-sex couples as it does to heterosexual ones. The push for marriage equality is a clear example of this.

Another interesting element of contemporary romance discourse is that it often conflates sex and love, a phenomenon that again, is relatively recent (Illouz 1997; de Botton 2006; Hayes et al. 2012). Up until the mid-eighteenth century – and arguably even later – there was a clear separation between love, sex and family (Coontz 2005; de Botton 2006).

> For its part, the impulse to raise a family has been well-known to the largest share of humanity since our earliest upright days in east Africa. In all this time, however, it seems to have occurred to almost no one (until very recently, evolutionarily speaking) that this project might need to be fused together with constant sexual desire as well as frequent sensations of romantic longing at the sight of our fellow parent across the breakfast table.
>
> (de Botton 2006: 118)

Is it too ambitious to think we can achieve all three through the one relationship? Branden (2008: xxiii) argues that love "is one of the great possibilities of our existence, one of the great adventures, and one of the great challenges", claiming that "it refuses to be extinguished because it answers profound human needs". This essentialized view of romantic love sounds tempting, but if we as humans have such "profound needs", why has romantic love only been discovered recently as the natural answer to those needs?

I suggest that it does indeed attempt to address some human needs, but those needs most probably are an artefact of our culture and economy more than any essential part of human nature. Perhaps we have evolved to the point where we are more emotionally and sexually developed, more articulate about what our needs are, and romantic love has evolved as the perfect answer. More likely, however, romantic love is merely a best-fit paradigm that is beginning to unravel because civilization, in its ever-evolving character, has changed to the point where the perfect answer is beginning to look quite flawed. Hence the amount of spaghetti we all carry around in our heads about it. Or perhaps civilization and technology have evolved to the point where distortions of love are allowed to occur unchecked or unnoticed. I suggest that it is not romantic love *per se*, or even the spaghetti surrounding it we have cause to be wary of. Rather, it may well be the perversities of romantic love and the ways in which it can be stretched out of proportion, bent and broken that should be cause for concern. In itself, romantic love has a lot going for it, including companionship, shared values, sexual fulfilment, emotional support and self-discovery (Branden 2008; Sioux 2011). It is when romantic love is misused to justify abuse and disrespect that it becomes dangerous. In the following chapters, we shall explore some of the ways in which love gets distorted and the impact that has on the individuals involved and on society in general. For the moment, though, I shall explore two more discourses – the first, pathologizing love, is pseudo-psychological; the second, the romancing of parental love, returns us back to enchantment from another angle.

Pathologizing love

There is an enormous market in self-help books on love and intimate relationships, ranging from how to hook the partner of your dreams, to how to get over a break-up, and everything in between.

A quick survey of an online bookstore conducted at the time of writing identified so many of these that I gave up counting after 200. This alone should convince us of the pervasiveness of romantic love in society, but there is more. I am now receiving spam emails about everything from how to attract a man, to how to control a woman, what makes women tick, what makes men tick and how to have great sex. Admittedly, I have had the junk filters on my email removed for research purposes, but the sheer amount of self-help information circulating on the internet is nothing short of astounding. Websites such as 2knowmyself.com and Wikihow.com share a wealth of information and tips about falling in love, finding your soul mate, coping with relationship problems, how to break up with someone, how to recover when someone breaks up with you and so on. The following surveys some of the more prominent and enduring tips and pieces of advice offered online.

M. Farouk Radwan, author of 2knowmyself.com, has produced a range of self-help e-books, one of which is titled, *How to Make Someone Fall in Love With You* (2008). He claims that his book is based on sound psychological theory, though he himself has no formal qualifications. Crudely, he claims that research is the key – get to know your potential love-object, then show her how much like her you are. People like to fall in love with people they can identify with. Once you've established a connection, do many memorable things together. Following Aron et al. (2007) above, Radwan argues that experiencing fun (or some other memorable experience) with someone, makes them more attracted to you.

Many of the tips about how to attract someone focus on being unavailable – the "we always want what we can't have" discourse mentioned earlier in this chapter. Under the heading "How to Make Someone Fall in Love With You" on wikihow.com, the following advice is offered:

> Be unavailable. It's human nature to want what we can't have. You shouldn't be rude or blow the other person off, but making yourself seem busy and full of other friends and projects will make you appear more desirable.[3]

Loveblab.com advises, "guys love a mystery", so don't tell him your entire life story on the first date. Be mysterious.[4] Along the same lines, a blog by Wicked Sago talks about the "law of scarcity", comparing love to economics:

> In economics, the law of scarcity states that if what you desire is in limited supply or seemingly limited supply, its perceived value increases. This also increases the urge for people to want it and want it immediately.[5]

This harks back to Bauman's (2008) point that in our "Liquid Society", we tend to think about relationships like shopping. Much like other commodities, love is about supply and demand – the more people want us, the higher our value, and the better deal we can make in a love match. The woman who could have any number of potential lovers because she is so beautiful/clever/rich/endearing is worth more to us as a partner because having her also increases our own worth in the market. A moment from my own dating history confirms this – upon finding out I had started dating a very popular person in my 20-something social group, one of my friends came up and said to me, "H left M for YOU?" – the implication that H could have done better did hurt, to an extent, but also afforded me a certain status in the group thereafter. Obviously there was something about me that others had failed to appreciate!

In spite of the parallels to shopping, counsel typically advises against standing in line waiting for Mr or Mrs Right. Squidoo.com suggests that you "let him chase you",[6] as well as keeping dates short so he'll want more. Notice that most of this advice is aimed at heterosexual women. When it comes to giving men advice, the focus is on how to attract a woman rather than how to make her love you. Many of the sites advise that women are most attracted to the "alpha male". Attractwomenbooks.com, for example, claims that, "in general every woman wants a **man**. More specifically the **alpha**, the chief of the tribe, the leader of the pack. And not the needy, weak, and the easily manipulated chump" (emphasis in original), and then, "sex appeal is fifty percent what you got and fifty percent what people think you got".[7] The focus on hegemonic masculinity consolidates the gendered discourse of self-help websites, which entreats women to be sexy but not needy, while advising men to be the "leader of the pack". In both cases, women and men alike are pathologized when it comes to relationships – don't be needy or weak, be confident and independent!

Apparently people in general have difficulty following this advice because there is also a plethora of websites and books offering insight into how to cope with unrequited love, how to keep a relationship going, and how to recover when someone breaks off a relationship with you. These sites focus on the pathology of love, drawing on traditional and folk psychology, positive thinking methodologies, assertiveness training and even addiction therapy. Clearly, romantic love and attraction occupy a huge role in hetero-sexual lives, yet so many are not coping with or are confused by the discourse.

With respect to non-heterosexuals and transgender individuals, there appear to be very few websites devoted exclusively to LGBT romance advice, although there are plenty of pornographic sites. Much of the advice that is available comes in the form of forums, dating sites and articles posted on LGBT-focused sites. However, the advice seems to mirror the heteronormative narrative. In an article on examiner.com, the writer advises lesbians that yes, even they are entitled to the perfect relationship:

> If you are single and you can't seem to "get it together" to reach your dream of being "settled in" with a woman you can build an exciting future with, what are you waiting for? I speak to too many single lesbians who complain of this fact.[8]

In many of the forums, lesbians discuss the difficulty of distin-guishing between friendship, attraction and love and this appears to complicate the pathology of love. Another issue is falling in love with a heterosexual friend, which compounds the unrequited love discourse because the relationship was never a possibility. The fol-lowing remark, made in a "Lesbian Relationship Challenges Support Group" forum, is common:

> I understand. My first love was the same...Met her in 2003, I couldn't tell her, as she was straight...It use [sic] to kill me see-ing her with someone else (specially as it was a guy). I was "best friend" to her...[9]

For gay men, infidelity appears to be the most common issue. A letter on thegaylovecoach.com states:

> I met my ex-boyfriend while living abroad and, according to him, it was love at first sight. Everything went wrong when we moved in with his parents. We would constantly fight, he became insanely jealous, we'd even get physical.
>
> On Christmas he decided to go on a trip with his friend. He met another guy who he had sex with. He accepted he cheated on me, but that wasn't the reason he didn't want to be with me anymore.[10]

The same site also offers the following advice to singles:

> The first step is to define your vision for your ideal partner and relationship when developing your dating goals for the New Year. What are the qualities you're seeking, and of those characteristics, which of those needs are negotiable versus deal-breakers?[11]

For both gay men and lesbians, the advice offered on many of the sites appears to be similar to the advice offered to heterosexual women, suggesting that notions of romantic love and long-term relationships have infiltrated the non-heterosexual community and suffer the same pathologies to a relatively similar extent, contributing to homonormativity.

Lesbians, in particular, seem prone to the romantic self-help ideology. Gay men, on the other hand, tend to gravitate towards pornographic and sex-related sites. One possible explanation is that women are well-trained in romance discourses and so assume that other women will feel as they do. Anecdotally, that often appears to be the case – two women with a bad case of romantic fluffiness must logically be double the trouble. The pathology of neediness, possessiveness and fusing of identity spreads across sexualities and genders and speaks to the pervasiveness of romantic love discourses in our society.

I would argue that it even spreads across other, non-erotic love relationships, that we romance some non-sexual relationships in many of the same ways. One particularly interesting example is the romancing of parental love.

Romancing parental love

It might seem to be stretching the point to connect romance with parental love, but as I will demonstrate, we adopt many of the romantic discourses outlined above in our relationships with our children. Indeed, parental love may be even more romanced than the average heterosexual relationship. Parents often literally fall in love with their children from birth, and continue to gush romantically about them until they reach puberty – often beyond. To date, there is no research or literature relating to romantic parenting, and so the following analysis is of necessity based on my observations of and musings on parental and family culture in popular media and culture. It does not pretend to be authoritative, but rather raises questions about the role of love in parenting, the relationship parents in Western society have with their children, and the intersectional implications of this. I appreciate that this analysis is purely speculative, but hope that it provides some insight into how we as Western parents relate to our children.

First and foremost, I want to point out the special place that children, and especially babies, have in the lives of modern affluent and semi-affluent families. How many parents have held their newborn baby for the first time and felt an overwhelming rush of feeling – a mixture of delight, affection, and incredulousness, leading to complete enchantment with and devotion to the child? No amount of dirty nappies, puking or crying can dampen the ardour of the truly infatuated parent. The infatuation continues through toddlerhood and into primary school. Many an infatuated parent has stood at the gates of their child's preschool and cried as they watch their precious baby wave goodbye on their first day. The first rudimentary strokes of pencil on paper, first teeth, locks of hair, innumerable photographs and other memorabilia are stowed away as precious treasures. Enormous amounts of money are spent on soft toys, building blocks, dolls, toy cars, cutesy clothes and gadgets; then later on electronic and computer equipment, mobile phones, books, bags, school trips, name brand shoes, clothes and toys (Faw 2012; Cornish 2013). No starry-eyed Romeo ever spoilt or gushed over his beloved so much as today's middle- and upper-class parents do their children.

I remember delighting in dressing up my daughter when she was a baby, crooning to her, stroking her cheek, cuddling her and thinking she was perfect. Living away from my parents and family, I discovered how to care for her through the many books available on the subject, from *What to Expect the First Year*, to *Toddler Training* and so on. Parental discourses are no less dominated by the self-help industry than other romantic love discourses. Parenting books and websites abound. Essentialbaby.com.au, for example, is littered with pictures of cute smiling babies wrapped in soft towels, and offers articles about every stage of growth and every issue involved in parenting, from breastfeeding to whether they should be using a dummy, to how to recognize when your baby has a headache.[12] Huggies.com.au sports a sleeping baby next to the headline: "perfection like never before deserves protection like never before".[13] Clearly, where we fail to find the perfect spouse, we get a second chance with our perfect baby.

Television shows, such as *Modern Family*, caricature these discourses, but they are careful to maintain their integrity and make them inclusive. Gay partners Mitchell and Cam adopt an Asian child in the first series, and proceed to gush, spoil and fawn over her every move and sound. Series such as *The Middle* and *Malcolm in the Middle* spoof this parental romancing, but they can do so only because they depict working-class families who cannot afford to romance their children the way Mitchell and Cam do. They want to give their children everything, but they are thwarted by lack of income, overburdening jobs, and school bullies.

Romantic parenting appears to be a fairly recent phenomenon, one that I suggest is symptomatic of the obsession our society has with romance and romantic love, not to mention youth, beauty and social status. Our children become a part of us in the same way our adult intimate partners do, but they also represent us and all that we stand for (Brummelman et al. 2013). Parental love is therefore, I would argue, edging towards a form of narcissism. Any failure of the child is reflected on the parent and many parents also live through their children, through their accomplishments, talents and aspirations, particularly where they were denied themselves in their youth (Brummelmann et al. 2013).

The rise of a specifically white, middle-class mode of romantic parenting appears to have begun early in the twentieth century and coincides with the rise of affluence leading to increased leisure and consumerism, in particular of film and television (Seiter 1995). Prior to that, at least from the eighteenth century onwards (Aries 1973), children were loved and cared for by parents and extended families and communities, but the rise of film exposed us to the idealization of the child (Newman and Smith 1999), most specifically in the invention of Shirley Temple and the notion of "cuteness" (Merrish 1996: 186). Young Shirley began her career at the age of three, and in 1934, at the age of four, achieved international fame in *Bright Eyes*, a film written especially for her, and which was closely followed by *Curly Top*, *Heidi*, and a long list of others. In each film she starred as the child ingénue and with her cute dimpled, smiling face and head full of ringlets, little baby doll dresses and tap shoes, she danced, sang and giggled her way into the hearts and minds of her adoring audience. She was the first celebrity to be merchandized through dolls, tea sets and clothes and she captured an entire generation (Klotman 1979: 124). When television became popular in the 1940s and 1950s, her films were some of the first and most popular to be shown.

They were still popular in the 1960s when I was growing up and I remember being glued to the television, enamoured by her talent and charm, along with that of Doris Day and Elvis Presley. For me she framed girlish perfection and undoubtedly contributed towards both my parents and my own views of femininity, girlhood and parental romanticizing. "Cuteness" became a culturally recognized sign of perfect childhood to which one was required to respond with "culturally specified normative emotions" (Merrish 1996: 186). Merrish (1996: 186) argues that adoring the cute child requires a "logic of identification" in which we embrace the cuteness as something we can identify with and want to be (or want our children to be). What little girl of my generation and the one before didn't want to be just like Shirley?

Doris Day and Elvis Presley, on the other hand, taught me all about romantic love of the adult kind. The line was fine, however. No one ever had sex in those early films, at least not in the ones I was allowed to watch, and so it took me some time to differentiate between the two kinds of romance. Indeed, it wasn't until the 1970s that film and television regularly featured couples in double beds, let alone being intimate. No doubt all this sexless romancing influenced entire generations, which is probably why young and middle-aged women alike have such trouble defining the boundaries of love and sex. In Chapter 5, I discuss this issue and the ways in which love and sex become separated in some contexts, while becoming conflated in others.

Love outside the heteronormative

Judging by the recent heavy campaigning across the globe for marriage equality, many same-sex and transgender couples want marriage equality and legal surrogacy so that they can set up nuclear households and raise children like their heterosexual counterparts. At the other end of the continuum lies "beats" and men who have sex with men, open relationships, polyamory and consensual sadomasochism, sex workers and adult entertainers (Barker 2012). The enchantment of romantic love is challenged by these "deviancies" because they demonstrate how people can flourish outside heteronormativity (and homonormativity) even in the face of outright legal and social discrimination and exclusion. However, although there is much scholarly debate about the topic (e.g. Bauman 2004; Weeks 2007; Halberstam 2013), I would argue that so far, these challenges are largely unheard and unnoticed by the general public.

Disney has produced several non-white princesses,[14] and even one that refused to get married,[15] but it has yet to have two princes or princesses fall in love. Some schools have books with stories of "Two Mummies" and television series such as *Modern Family* make gay families respectable, but only because they conform to the loving, monogamous family paradigm. *Queer as Folk* came closer to challenging homonormativity than *Glee*, but in the end it too succumbed to the romantic love discourse as well as to stereotypes of LGBT characters and the loving couple discourse, as did *The L Word*. Clearly, that which challenges the hetero- or homo-normative must remain invisible, relegated to specific spaces, accessed in the shadows of everyday culture where it cannot corrupt families or offend the mainstream.

Conclusion

This chapter has explored the ways in which contemporary discourses about romantic love influence our understandings and expectations of relationships. There is clear evidence of pathologies and contradictions – between romance and marriage, between deviance and normativity, between adult love and parental love, and between love and sex. These contradictions impact the ways in which we engage in meaningful relationships, understand and apply the notion of love, and reveal that the more glaring are the contradictions, the more tenaciously we appear to stick to them. Zigmunt Bauman (2003) argues that these contradictions necessarily arise out of our "Liquid Society", which is characterized, among other things, by

> ... [t]he uncanny frailty of human bonds, the feeling of insecurity that frailty inspires, and the conflicting desires that feeling prompts to tighten the bonds yet keep them loose....
>
> (Bauman 2003: viii)

Bauman (2013: L107) argues that Liquid Society treats relationships like networks, thereby missing the essential merits of connectedness: "Network stands for a matrix of simultaneously connecting and disconnecting. In a network, connections can be entered on demand, and can be broken at will." Thus, we are faced with a logic of non-recursive relationships that promises enduring intimacy, while at the same time preventing it by creating the conditions for conflict and separation. Desire and romance thwart each other:

> Desire is the crush to consume... and is therefore an urge to destruction. Desire is contaminated from its birth by the death wish... Love is, on the other hand, the wish to care, and to preserve the object of the care... [It is a] centrifugal urge to expand.
>
> (Bauman 2003: 9)

Romance confuses and conflates love with desire and is therefore inherently contradictory. It is also intimately connected to specific identities and subjectivities, the nature of experience and the role of representation in social life (Weatherall 1995). Sioux (2011) argues that this logic is underpinned by the addictive euphoria experienced when romantic love is encountered. Perhaps it is the addictive nature of romance that fuels the continued acceptance of these contradictions, or perhaps it is due to the fact that these discourses are implanted in our psyche. Chapter 3 explores the impact of romantic discourses further through an analysis of media, film and popular culture depictions of romantic love and the ways in which these distort our views of love, relationships and femininity.

3
From Disney to Distortion[1]

Introduction

This chapter explores how media depictions of femininity and romantic love impact culture and influence the way we think about gender and relationships. The mass marketing of films such as the *Twilight* series and the Disney Princesses franchise, for example, illustrates how seemingly innocuous storylines and characters idealize pain, tragedy, and sacrifice as necessary and acceptable components of romantic love. This chapter will explore how such phenomena distort our perceptions and expectations of intimate relationships, creating cultural narratives around the inevitability of, and transformative power of, abuse. This chapter also analyses media influence on young girls and boys, especially with respect to their self-esteem, and perceptions of body image and gender normativity. It will explore media representations of gender and gendered bodies and how these contribute to the development of hegemonic stereotypes. The term "young girls and boys" includes pre-school, pre-pubescent and pubescent children.

I have already discussed in some depth in Chapter 1 the impact of the *Twilight* film series on our discourses of romantic love. This chapter, therefore, focuses on another important cinematic source of influence – the Disney Princess films. First, it explores and analyses the impact of these films on gender and sexuality norms and subjectivities, focusing particularly on how the discourses generated from them govern girls and young women. It then moves on to examine the ways in which intimate relationships are depicted in the films, and the impact of discourses of love and romance.

Sexualization and media

The sexualization of girls is a much-researched phenomenon in the scholarly literature, and I do not intend to rehearse those arguments here. Rather, I will explore the notion of sexualization in terms of media influence as a vehicle for analysing gendered constructs of romantic love that arguably tolerate, if not actually lead to, abuse. My analysis of these constructs identifies underlying misogynistic themes that are, paradoxically, both insidious and obvious – on the one hand unrecognized or unacknowledged, while on the other, used in blatant resistance against such constructs.

The word "sexualization" can be broadly understood as giving a person or object a sexual character, making an object or person appear sexual, or using a person's sexuality to sell something (Rush and La Nauze 2006; Egan 2013). The notion of sexualization may be constructed in both positive and negative terms, depending on context. The two key positions in the literature regard sexualization as either intrinsically harmful or as the cause of moral panic (Egan 2013). Advocates of the former accuse the moral panic theorists of being "de-sensitized to the issue", while the latter depict the intrinsically harmful advocates as "hysterical, religious, neo-liberal or only trying to save the image of the white, middle-class, heterosexual tween-aged girl" (Rush and La Nauze 2006; Lumby and Albury 2010; Egan 2013). Despite these contrasting viewpoints, both agree that the sexualization of young girls is a contemporary phenomenon, whether for better or worse (Egan 2013). My own analysis suggests that, while there may indeed be some level of cultural paranoia surrounding the issue, there is genuine cause for concern regarding its long-term impact on all genders, and in relationships in general, not necessarily from sexualization itself, but rather from the subjectivities that arise from it.

The Disney Princess franchise is a potent example of the enormous influence of media on young people (Orenstein 2011; Egan 2013). According to Disney's website, there are ten "official" Princesses – although at the time of writing, there is extensive media advertising for a new Disney Princess film, *Frozen*, and future Princesses will no doubt be added regularly. The current official heroines include Ariel, Aurora, Belle, Cinderella, Jasmine, Mulan, Pocahontas, Rapunzel, Snow White and Tiana (Disney/Pixar nd.). These characters were originally based on fairy tales, folk tales and historical characters dating as far back as the sixth century (Orenstein 2011; World of Tales nd.). However, the stories surrounding them have in many cases changed quite dramatically to cater to a contemporary audience. The character of Jasmine, for example, is based on Princess Badroulbadour from the early nineteenth century folk tale *Aladdin and the Magical Lamp*, set in Persia and China. Princess Badroulbadour met Aladdin on her wedding night to another man, when Aladdin, who was described as being "violently in love" with the Princess, made a wish that made her bed magically appear. In the folk tale, she recounts her first encounter with Aladdin as "the most miserable night of her life". (Lang 1918; World of Tales 2013). Disney Jasmine, on the other hand, is happily swept away by Aladdin and, indeed, lives "happily ever after". Similarly, the character of Ariel, the youngest and most beautiful of six mermaid Princesses, originated in 1837 in Hans Christian Andersen's *Den lille Havfrue* (The Little Mermaid). The little Mermaid was 15 when she first saw the 16-year-old Prince, who she rescued from a sinking ship. She immediately fell in love and wished to marry the Prince, but discovered she would require an immortal soul and human legs, both of which only true love could provide. In attempting to win the Prince's love, the Mermaid sacrificed her fish tail and had her tongue cut out. She was told that, as a result, every step taken on land would feel like treading on knife blades and if the Prince rejected her, she would turn into sea foam. In the end, the Prince married another Princess and the little Mermaid threw herself off a ship to her fate (Andersen 1837; World of Tales 2013). Again, the Disney version sees Ariel and her Prince marrying and living happily ever after. The early folk tales were graphic and violent, designed to scare children into behaving according to conventional morality. They were meant to convey moral lessons about pride, covetousness, greed and envy. The Disney versions provide much watered-down story lines, virtually erasing all but the most superficial "lessons" for young children (Orenstein 2011). However, it is Disney's adaptations of these fairy tales that have been immortalized in film and are today regarded as authoritative.

The first Disney Princess film, *Snow White and the Seven Dwarfs*, was released over 80 years ago in 1937, decades before most of the other Princess movies (IMDB 1998). It wasn't until 2000 that Disney decided to combine the most popular female characters from a collection of Disney movies into the Princess franchise in order to capture a niche market (Orenstein 2011; Disneymedia nd.). Disney's advertising campaign is specifically designed to engage young girls and encourage them to identify with the individual Princesses (Disneymedia nd.). It is doubtful that even Disney executives foresaw the impact of the franchise, which quickly became a focus of obsessional consumerism by girls and their parents (Kilbourne and Levin 2008; Walter 2010; Disney 2011). Interestingly, Disney never targeted young boys as an audience for these films, in spite of evidence that shows that young boys like to dress up and play out roles just as much as girls (Knesz 2007; Bryan 2012). Traditionally, of course, boys have been dressed in stereotypically masculine roles such as cowboys and "Indians", firemen, doctors, builders, or else superheroes such as Batman, Superman and so on, and these roles do not seem to fit with the Disney fairy tale mold. There is no equivalent franchise for Disney Princes although there is a significant market in "action toys" for boys, which focus on characters such as Buzz Lightyear from *Toy Story*, and Iron Man from the series of the same name. Arguably, the marketing of these toys have just as much impact on the development of gender norms for boys as the Disney Princesses appear to have for girls, and this will be discussed in Chapter 6. However, this chapter aims to explore female gender norms and how they are perceived by both boys and girls and so it will focus solely on the impact of media and corporate merchandising on girls.

Since the establishment of the Princess brand in 2000, Disney has seen a profit of over 4 billion dollars in global revenue (Disney 2011). In the USA alone, Disney Princesses are the top-selling licensed toy brand among girls of all ages, and the number one franchise for girls aged between two and five (Disney 2011; Orenstein 2011). Items marketed under the brand include multi-vitamins, strawberry yoghurt, tissues, cutlery, dining sets, tea pots, children's furniture, drink bottles, magazines, books, music, stationary, replica princess dolls, puzzles, replica costumes, cubby houses, kites, video games, and clothing (Disney Store nd.). It is almost impossible for most young girls not to own a few Disney Princess items (Walter 2010; Orenstein 2011).

According to the Disney website, "there is a Princess inside every little girl" and their goal is to enable them to "live the fantasy every moment of everyday" (Disney/Pixar 2013a). Disney claims that the

Princesses are simply harmless fun, engaging fantasies that encourage children to use their imaginations (Egan 2013). However, there is evidence to suggest that its impact is much more insidious (Orenstein 2011).

Childhood and gender

As noted in Chapter 2, historically children were seen as miniature adults, expected to work as soon as they were able, to be relatively independent and to contribute to the family economy (Aries 1973; Oakley 2004; Hayes et al. 2012). It was not until the sixteenth century that childhood was constructed as an individual developmental stage. However, the notion that children were innocent, vulnerable and in need of special protection did not become popular until the late eighteenth/early nineteenth century, which is why we see periods in history when child labour and child brides were socially acceptable (Aries 1973; Oakley 2004; Hayes et al. 2012). In the latter half of the nineteenth century, there was a shift in attitudes towards children, who came to be seen as unique, innocent and vulnerable to corruption (Aries 1973; Oakley 2004). This notion of childhood is endemic in Western society, which regards children as in need of special protection. This is evident in the United Nations *Convention of the Rights of the Child*, which highlights that "childhood is entitled to special care and assistance" (UN Committee on the Rights of the Child 2013).

The anti-sexualization debate focuses on the most vulnerable stages of childhood development for young girls, including pre-school, pre-pubescent and tween-age, which ranges between three and 14 years of age (Davis 2004). The term "tweenage" or "tweenager" refers to the period of time between children coming out of middle childhood and into adolescence, which is roughly between nine and 14 years of age, a time when they are experiencing a unique and influential period of sexual, cognitive and social development (Mersch nd).

Psychological models of child development typically focus on physical, social and neurological development, and claim that this period is developed around medico-social age and milestone markers that help determine whether a child is developing according to current norms (Davis 2004). Despite what some scholars suggest, it has been argued quite convincingly that children are not asexual beings (Davis 2004; Kellogg 2010). Research demonstrates that it is "developmentally appropriate" for pre-school age children to have heightened curiosity in sexuality and the human body (Davis 2004). Just how much of these models is a social construction mediated by power relations that work to govern families and children is debatable. Clearly, children do develop according to some sort of logic, although what is "normal" at any age is just the statistical mean. Nevertheless, there is ample evidence to suggest that young children are (and probably always have been) curious about their sexuality and genitalia (Aries 1989; Davis 2004). Therefore, it is difficult to justify the argument that access to media content sexualizes pre-school age children, although it is clear that such media do influence their development of gender identities. I suspect it is the physical expression of sexuality through the wearing of adult clothing, as well as erotic ways of moving and behaving that are the issue. If this is the case, then the Disney Princesses are relatively innocent, as they hardly rival the moves and attire of a Miley Cyrus or a Lady Gaga in action. What the Princesses may contribute to, however, is the heteronormalizing of girls through clothing and physicality. It is in her first Disney Princess film that a young girl will first watch and learn how a female should act and dress, how she should look, what her demeanour should be, and where she should direct her gaze. While a Prince will walk with purpose and speak directly, a Princess swishes and swirls, especially if she is wearing her gown and heels, and she speaks shyly – and more often than not, only when she is spoken to.

As they transition into pre-pubescence and pubescence (8–14), children are likely to become acutely aware of, and begin to imitate peer group normativities, gender roles and behaviours (Davis 2004). Children also may begin to imagine themselves in adult roles, often imitating their parents and other significant role models (Davis 2004). By the time children leave middle childhood for puberty, they become highly conscious of social pressures and expectations among their peer group (Davis 2004). Like adults, children construct their views of the world based on their observations and experiences (England et al. 2011). Thus the internal and external environments in which children develop can have a lasting impact on their subjective identities, and while parents have some control over their child's home environment, what children are exposed to outside the home in peer groups, education, sport and media is much more difficult to monitor. This reinforces the importance of understanding the impact that protracted exposure to the Disney Princess brand and the socially constraining ideas they represent, on young girls in particular (Davis 2004; Orenstein 2011).

Gender roles are learned by engaging with temporally dependent, socially constructed images and ideals presented by media, social groups and other role models (Bandura 1971; Haslanger and Sveinsdóttir 2011). Despite the evidence supporting the social construction of gender (Butler 1990; Schneider et al. 2005; Walter 2010), some academics continue to claim that there are genetic markers in the female and male brains that distinguish between the biological sexes, explaining, for example, why girls are drawn to pink and boys to blue, or why women are better suited to nurturing occupations such as teachers and nurses, and men to doctors or lawyers (Walter 2010; Orenstein 2013). Indeed, these so-called genetic characteristics are held to be definitive by large sections of the population of Western society, particularly those coming from a conservative political viewpoint. Australian Prime Minister, Tony Abbott, is famously reported to endorse this view when he commented, "I think it would be folly to expect that women will ever dominate or even approach equal representation in a large number of areas simply because their aptitudes, abilities and interests are different for physiological reasons."

Apart from the evidence against the theory of genetic markers, it is highly unlikely that genetic predisposition could be the only reason girls are drawn to pink dolls and boys are drawn to blue trucks. There is no doubt that toy companies draw on popular images and ideals that reinforce what society believes to be "normal" (Walter 2010). Gender role characteristics marketed to children have become increasingly more polarized and inflexible; the colour pink has become synonymous with little girls and blue with little boys (Levin and Kilbourne 2008; Walter 2010). However, literature demonstrates that children only became associated with particular colours in the twelfth century. Prior to that, they were generally dressed in gender-neutral white for convenience and hygiene (Orenstein 2011). Historically, the association of colour with gender was reversed; pink was considered to be more masculine and blue more feminine (Orenstein 2011). Pink was seen as "a pastel version of red...associated with strength" and blue was associated with "the Virgin Mary, constancy and faithfulness, symbolised femininity" (Orenstein 2011: 35).

In line with this, early female Disney characters wore shades of blue; for example, Mary Poppins, Cinderella, Alice in Wonderland and Sleeping Beauty all wore blue dresses (Orenstein 2011). In the late eighties, however, a clearly gender-defined colour code appeared in advertising and children's products. According to Orenstein (2011: 36), this was a direct result of a "dominant children's marketing strategy". Today, aisles of stores devoted to "girls" toys and clothing are saturated with pink, which has now become identified with and representative of the feminine (Walter 2010; Orenstein 2011).

The manner in which Disney defines beauty and gender roles also impacts young girls. Princess merchandise is marketed almost entirely to pre-school and pre-pubescent girls, who are most susceptible to external and peer influence (Davis 2004; Oakley 2004; Disney 2011; Orenstein 2011). Perceptions of beauty are highly subjective and differ vastly between cultures, but cultural normativities of beauty always have a powerful impact (Mallon 2008). Globalization and the rapid expansion of technology is fast enabling a collision between cultural perceptions of beauty, and it appears that Western ideals have, as usual, dominated (Luo 2012). The Western ideal of feminine beauty requires that women's bodies be thin, ageless, have big breasts and no imperfections (Wolf 2002; Elliot 2008). Apart from Mulan, who maintains a more Asian appearance, all the Disney Princesses, regardless of their cultural origin, overwhelmingly fit this dominant Western ideal.

The development of a sense of identity and socio-cultural belonging is an important task of childhood and adolescent learning (Titzmann 2012). Individuals model their social and cultural identities on dominant representations of cultural values (Luo 2012; Titzmann 2012). Such representations are influenced by the relationship between the individual and the cultural, religious and gender groups to which they belong (Titzmann 2012). Young girls imitate their peers and family members, who are keenly aware of the parameters of culturally acceptable bodily ideals (Davis 2004; Ching 2007). The manner in which the media presents women therefore influences the way young girls view themselves and what is perceived as "normal". Being a woman has become largely all about how she looks, her physicality, how she inhabits her body and uses language and voice. Her mind, her character, her spirituality all become secondary. This poses a problem for all girls, but especially for non-Western children and those who have alternate ethnic heritage, because "normal" most often depicts white, middle class, and with Caucasian facial features. The Western ideal thereby works to limit and restrict these children's sense of self and belonging (Disney 2011; Orenstein 2011; Tizmann 2012). In Disney films depicting non-Western or ethnically diverse characters, their physical traits have evolved from their original ethnic heritage to fit Western ideals of beauty and femininity. Some of the adaptations have also omitted essential cultural values associated with the particular ethnicity, as well as glossing over the harsher moral lessons of the original story, completely changing their intended purpose. As stated earlier, in the original story of Aladdin, Princess Badroulbadour wore a veil, her first marriage was arranged and the story implies that Aladdin kidnaps and rapes her (Lang 1918; World of Tales 2013). In the Disney adaptation, Princess Jasmine does not wear a veil, is not modestly dressed and certainly not raped.

Despite their rich ethnic heritage, Disney characters uniformly lack any clear non-Western or ethnic characteristics, unless they are cast as problematic minorities or villains (Foote 2012). The Princesses themselves present uniformly with slim physique, long hair and small, symmetrical features (Orenstein 2011). Even the non-Western Princesses are Westernized, their dress and demeanour adjusted accordingly. Princess Jasmine, for example, remains unveiled in clear opposition to her cultural origin (Lang 1918). The over-reliance on superficial, heavily doctored and stereotypical indicators of culture such as almond-shaped eyes, dark hair and olive skin, while omitting important traditional values, actual physical characteristics and attire, serves to make cultural differences invisible. This, in turn, minimalizes the importance of cultural identity to the young children who idolize the Princesses, potentially influencing the formation of their notions of self and subjectivity (Wolf 1993; Mallon 2008; Titzmann 2012). Thus, while the Disney stereotypes restrict Western Caucasian girls' expectations regarding appearance and behaviour, young girls of different cultural backgrounds are also restricted in their ability to express themselves culturally (Orenstein 2011; Foote 2012). Despite every effort to adorn themselves in Cinderella's attire, girls who are not white, as Foote (2012: 14) points out, may have "the dress, but not the skin, eyes, or hair colour or style".

Constructing bodies

As noted above, it has been argued that sexually suggestive marketing and advertising campaigns targeting children are a major cause of early sexualization (Rush and La Nauze 2006; Egan 2013). Contemporary corporate encouragement of children to imitate adults clearly contradicts the commonly held perception of children as innocent and vulnerable. We encourage young girls to dress as "imitation adults" and engage "in a highly sexualized popular culture", thereby enabling children to become "objects of desire while at the same time being objects of taboo" (Hayes et al. 2012: 16). This contradiction causes much confusion among young girls regarding what is expected and acceptable as a child. Concern has been raised about the potential sexual stimulation these images will bring to predators (Rush and La Nauze 2006; Lumby 2010; Tankard Reist 2010). However, Lumby (2010: 7) argues that to judge every image "through the eyes of the potential paedophile" is to succumb too readily to cultural paranoia. This is where the two sides of the debate clash; is society responsible for the protection of the child from all potential risks of harm, including images in the media, or is child protection limited to the contextual situation and the individual interpretation of those images? Additionally, such arguments place the onus on the potential child victims rather than the predators, which is misdirected at the very least – as paedophiles will abuse children regardless of what they are wearing – and harmful at worst, because such arguments work to remove or hamper children's sense of safety and of being secure in the world.

While the argument around what exactly constitutes sexualization and sexualized images remains unsolved, the impacts of gender role socialization on the psychological development of young girls and the negative health impacts this causes, for example body image and self-esteem issues, are widely agreed upon (Wolf 1991; Orenstein 2011). There is ample research on the impact of consistent media exposure to unrealistic stereotypes on young girls growing up in Western cultures, demonstrating strong links between body image and substantially declining levels of self-esteem

(Egan 2013). According to the Australian Psychological Society (APS) (2013) "...society's idealization of thinness and the 'perfect' body as synonymous with beauty and success" is one of the major contributing factors for individuals, especially girls, developing eating disorders (APS 2013). The Australian government also recognizes that the way popular media portrays physical beauty can influence the body image pressures young people experience (Commonwealth of Australia 2009).

It has been argued that the idealization of feminine stereotypes in the media also precipitates self-destructive behaviours, including negative body image issues, anxiety, low self-esteem, self-harm and depression (Wolf 1993; Tankard Reist 2010; Orestein 2011). The psychological research shows that individuals with low self-esteem, who are perfectionists and sensitive to criticism, are considered more susceptible to depression (Beyond Blue 2009). Critics of this argument, however, question just how much impact these images have on girls and issues such as self-harm and depression, which obviously have complex causation (Lumby 2010; Egan 2013). The fact that not all girls are affected to such an extent also raises questions about the importance of the impact of idealized feminine stereotypes (Lumby 2010; Egan 2013).

However, it is clear that many young girls emulate and identify with Disney Princesses, and that the princesses portray unrealistic and racially discriminatory stereotypes (Levin and Kilbourne 2008; Walter 2010). Along with Disney Princesses, young girls also model themselves on Barbie and Bratz dolls, which similarly portray artificial and unrealistic ideals of beauty (Walter 2010; Orestein 2011). Many girls want to grow up to be a Princess, a fantasy that is encouraged by parents, who pander to the "cuteness" ideal, and which is made possible by the extensive availability of Disney branded merchandise (Walter 2010; Disney/Pixar 2013). While the Disney phase usually wears off by age nine or ten (if not earlier), its impact is already well-ingrained by the time girls reach puberty.

Teenagers tend to gravitate towards role models who are singers and celebrities, such as Miley Cyrus, Lady Gaga, Paris Hilton and Victoria Beckham (Levin and Kilbourne 2008; Walter 2010). Walter (2010: 3) suggests that these role models "...take the plastic look so far that they seem to have been created by Mattel". When media portrayals of the "ideal" female body appear to be unattainable, even through diet, exercise and cosmetics, girls who do not fit the norm are set up for failure (Wolf 1993). It is for that reason that these negative images and gender stereotypes have been directly linked to body image issues including low self-esteem, eating disorders, depression and anxiety (Wolf 1993; Orenstein 2011). Reportedly, in today's consumer culture, low self-esteem and depression are common even among primary school girls, who face enormous pressure to emulate these normativities (Dodge 1993; Clay et al. 2005). Children with low self-esteem and depression also are more prone to bullying and victimization (Jensen-Campbell et al. 2009). The pressures of not conforming to socially acceptable ideals of beauty, body and gender can result in much torment for the girl who is not thin, white, big-breasted, or traditionally "pretty" (Orenstein 2011). Moreover, knowing that one is judged first and foremost by one's physicality may stymie any inclination to develop intellectually, emotionally and spiritually. The dominance of physicality in contemporary popular culture must therefore necessarily lead to an intellectually and emotionally impoverished generation of women, if it hasn't already.

Governing bodies through policy

The way that legislation governs bodies and genders is also instructive. In the state of Queensland, Australia, where I live, the *Child Protection Act 1999* (s9) defines harm to the child, as " ... any detrimental effect of a significant nature on physical, psychological or emotional well-being" (Queensland government 2013), a definition that, like that in most other Western nations, takes its mark from dominant global values. The United Nations Children's Fund (UNICEF) (2012: 2) recently released a set of child safety principles directed at businesses, stating that, "childhood is a unique period of rapid physical and psychological development, during which young people's physical, mental and emotional health and well-being can be permanently affected for better or worse". Exposure to harmful and unrealistic images has the potential to affect young girls (and boys) later in life, making it necessary to monitor their exposure to these images (Davis 2004; UNICEF 2005). UNICEF (2005: 27) recognizes the potential long-term harms of "sexualization" and stereotypes in the media and outlines in the sixth principle that businesses should be aware of a child's "...greater susceptibility to manipulation, and the effects of using unrealistic or sexualized body images and stereotypes".

The Australian government has provided voluntary guidelines for the media industry, through the *"Voluntary Industry Code of Conduct on Body Image"*, which outlines fundamental areas of improvement required to promote long-term change aiming at healthy body image and realistic concepts of beauty (Commonwealth of Australia 2012b). One of the principles suggests that the media adopt and promote realistic and natural images of women, instead of digitally altered, unnatural and unattainable images (Commonwealth of Australia 2012b). The principle also suggests that corporations and advertisers ensure that the public is aware when images have been manipulated (Commonwealth of Australia 2012b).

Romance Disney-style

Media depictions of femininity and romantic love impact culture and influence the way we think about gender and relationships. We have already seen how the mass marketing of the Disney Princesses franchise impacts girls' constructions of gender and self-identity. However, a close analysis of the franchise also illustrates how seemingly innocuous storylines and characters idealize pain, tragedy and sacrifice as necessary and acceptable components of romantic love. Chapter 2 has already explored how the character of Belle in *Beauty and the Beast* succumbs to this distorted view of relationships. This section will explore how such phenomena twist our own perceptions and expectations of intimate relationships, creating cultural narratives around the inevitability of, and transformative power of, abuse.

Popular narratives of romantic love depicted in Disney films, as well as films such as *Twilight* and *The Time Traveller's Wife*, mirror the narratives which we hear from victims of domestic abuse and teen relationship violence (Sioux 2011). Sioux (2011) likens the *Twilight* films to "female crack cocaine". Edward Cullen's natural instinct as a vampire is to consume human blood, and Bella's blood especially calls to him like heroin to an addict. In spite of his natural instinct to destroy, however, he does not want her to become like him, and in that sense refuses to give in to his natural instinct. Both he and Bella (and the film and book audiences) interpret his attraction to her as romantic love, thus tying the will to destroy to the passionate and erotic. "He can't help his natural instinct to want to destroy Bella even though he doesn't really want to" (Sioux 2011: 55). His behaviour is not just acceptable, it's romantic because he sacrifices his deepest instinct for her sake. He can't help his instincts because he is damaged, turned immortal and predator against his will. Bella can save him from his fate by loving him. Bella's death at his hands, claims Sioux (2011: 56) is evidence of the mingling of the erotic and the tragic, where "erotic and passionate love" meets "violence and pain". This narrative makes victims of women, and victimhood romantic.

This valorisation of victimhood and the tragedy of romantic love provide at least some explanation for why women and girls enter into and stay in abusive relationships. Disney distorts what love looks like, what it should feel like and misrepresents the cues and signals that girls should be looking for. Our love culture teaches girls they can change and control the feelings of a man. We often believe we can make them love us.

> The self-defeat, the sacrifice, the giving up of self is in our feminine collective dialogue, and it is like crack cocaine to us.... We tell ourselves that doing self-defeating things for a man is romantic.... Her [Bella's] story – our story – feeds the rapists, child molesters, girlfriend and wife batterers. The fairytales we read our daughters at night groom them to believe in a really distorted and dangerous definition of love.
>
> (Sioux 2011: 80)

Wood (2001) refers to these dialogues as "dark romance narratives" that are "culturally legitimated" through the perpetuation and acceptance of the inevitability of violence in romantic love. Prince Charming is no less controlling and dominating than the Prince of Darkness, because when a woman's self-worth is "inextricably tied to having a male partner", it matters not whether he is good or bad – indeed, the bad boy lover and partner is possibly one of the most sought-after stereotypes. And such stereotypes are not confined to fairy tales, films and Disney Princesses. A recent advertisement by Dolce and Gabbana depicts a beautifully groomed young woman wearing a very skimpy, sexy (D&G) gown and stilettos, being held down by a very good-looking, shirtless young man, while several other similarly handsome, buff men look on. She does not look like she's enjoying herself; rather, she looks resigned, almost blank or numb. The fact that the photo depicts five big men looking like they're about to rape her suggests that this is just another day in the life of the woman, something to be expected. Violence is not only thereby normalized, it is applauded, because after all, she is lucky to have the attention of such obviously desirable men. The violent nature of the pose combined with the way the subjects are presented suggests that violence and domination are sexy. This is not simple BDSM (which is at least arguably consensual) – this is gang rape.

Images such as this one serve to normalize male need and female passivity and compliance. As O'Brien et al. (2013: 23) state: "such acceptance of gendered sexual performances are embedded in cultural norms about sexuality and reflect gendered stereotypes and behavioural expectations" in which "traditional masculine roles prioritise independence, assertiveness and sexual exploration and traditional feminine roles prioritise passivity and virtue..." (O'Brien et al. 2013). This observation appears to be borne out in the research on domestic abuse. Sugarman and Frankel (1996, cited in Wood 2001: 244), for example, concluded that "women who tolerate assault from husbands held more traditionally feminine identities than those who were not assaulted". Add to this the economic imperative of weddings and family life still so deeply ingrained in our society, and it is clear that the Disney Princess fantasy of married life is extremely difficult to dislodge, even in the face of consistent abuse. Berlant (2011: 4) argues that we as a society have been caught up in a kind of cruel optimism, in which the retraction of the Western fantasy of "the social democratic promise of the post second World War period in the US and Europe," characterized by upward mobility, job security, political and social equality, and lively durable intimacy, dies hard. The concept of "life-building" provides the "discourses of control" via which the "processes and procedures involved historically in the administration of law and bodies" are endlessly reproduced, making it well-nigh impossible to step outside of it (Berlant 2011: 93).

While Berlant's argument might be somewhat overstated, it echoes Foucault's (1982) observations about the uses of biopower, which is "the power to regulate life, the authority to force living not just to happen, but to endure and appear in particular ways". Romantic love and gendered stereotypes perpetuate a logic "where living increasingly becomes a scene of the administration, discipline and recalibration of what constitutes health" (Berlant 2011: 97). Relationship and family health is characterized by enduring intimacy, partnership and loyalty. For many women, there is no competing narrative on which to draw to explain abuse and violence, and therefore no expectation that they may become free of it – or that they are even entitled to become free of it. In her work on the normalization of violence in heterosexual relationships, Julia Wood (2001: 239) interviewed 20 women from ex-violent relationships and found that "women's use of gender and romance narratives to make sense of violent relationships legitimized both fairytale and dark romance narratives".

Conclusion

Watching a Disney Princess or *Twilight* film occasionally may be completely innocuous; however, Orenstein and others argue that there is a harmful cumulative impact, especially when stereotypical images of femininity and masculinity lead to negative body image and distorted perceptions of relationships (Walter 2010; Orenstein 2011). Corporate-led consumption of children's products that promote negative and unhealthy messages, advertised directly to children in a way they cannot fully understand or consent to, has been referred to as "corporate paedophilia" (Rush and La Nauze 2006). The saturation and extensive availability of Disney Princesses merchandise makes Disney a core contributor (Rush and La Nauze 2006; Walter 2010; Orenstein 2011; Disney/Pixar 2013b). While it seems rather extreme to suggest that the sexualization of girls through the media may promote paedophilia, the notion that transnational corporations such as Disney practice corporate-led consumption does not (Lumby and Albury 2010; Egan 2013). Clearly, the ubiquitousness of the Princess franchise not only impacts young girls' formation of their self-identity and ways of relating to the world and to boys and men, it is also a symptom of the broader governance of both individuals and society through consumerism and the economic imperative.

The cumulative impact of these films also influences the ways in which young girls frame intimate relationships and their roles within them. When female characters are presented as passive, nervous, fearful, and bashful, they reinforce the seeming normality of the infantalized woman who never leaves girlhood behind. The "ritual of subordination" reiterated in these films is non-verbal as well as verbal, submissiveness and powerlessness depicted in the way female characters pose, gaze and move (Media Education Foundation 2011). This feeds into the popular culture ideal of romantic love, which is characterized by men's "urge to protect, feed, shelter, caress, cosset and pamper, jealously guard" and women's "being in service" (Bauman 2003: 9–10). It speaks to the need to surrender to love and possession. I quote Bauman again:

> If desire wants to consume, love wants to possess. While the fulfillment of desire is coterminous with the annihilation of its object, love grows with its acquisitions and is fulfilled in their durability.
>
> (Bauman 2003: 10)

It is the surrender to and possessiveness of romantic love that feeds the distorted view of relations for people of all genders. As Ivan Kilma points out, "there is little that comes so close to death as fulfilled love" (cited in Bauman 2003). The next chapter explores how the distortion of romantic love makes abusive relationships difficult to decipher and subsequently deal with.

4
From Distortion to Abuse

Introduction

This chapter seeks to explore the relation between discourses of romantic love and women's acceptance of abuse in relationships. Elsewhere, I have argued that relationship abuse is not only a problem for women in heterosexual relationships (Hayes and Jeffries 2013) and there is much research demonstrating that female victimization by both male and female partners occurs across the spectrum of sexualities (e.g. see Mouzos and Makkai 2004; Pitts et al. 2006; Johnson et al. 2007; Ball and Hayes 2010). Domestic abuse has

> negative and long-lasting costs to female survivors including physical ill health, increased levels of anxiety, depression, fear, feelings of incompetence, eating and sleeping disorders, increased misuse of drugs and alcohol, loss of self esteem, elevated feelings of insecurity, general loss of quality of life and damaged life opportunities.
>
> (Hayes and Jeffries 2013)

Nevertheless, many women stay with or find it difficult to leave their abusive partners. This chapter explores the alternative discourses available to women in abusive relationships and how various discourses impact women's decisions to stay with or leave their partners. In doing so, I canvass a range of feminist, psychological and political discourses as well as the lived experience of victims through their stories of abuse and their efforts at leaving the situation. These stories were gleaned from publicly available websites devoted to supporting victims of domestic abuse, including online discussion forums. In this way I hope to present some understanding of how women's discursive experiences are linked to discourses of romantic love, health, and gender.

Dominant discourses

In earlier research conducted with Samantha Jeffries (Hayes and Jeffries 2013), I examined the discourses available to women that they might use to explain their abuse. A common theme in the scholarly literature is that for survivors of abuse, the ability to name and understand their experiences can be liberating. Whether, how and in what ways women come to recognize their abuse as such and then make decisions with regard to their relationships appeared to be dependent on their ability to find alternative discourses to those traditionally associated with romantic love. We identified four key discourses used by women to make sense of their abuse and assist them to disengage from their partners: the first and most accessed is the discourse of patriarchy; the second and third are psychological discourses – one of victims and one of offenders; and the fourth, the discourse of romantic love. We found that the discourse of romantic love was most likely to keep women in abusive relationships, while the psychological offender discourse was most likely to aid in disengagement (Hayes and Jeffries 2013).

Unfortunately this psychological offender discourse, which generally identifies the abuser as severely damaged in some way that is neither the woman's responsibility nor in her capacity to heal, is not widely available. While there are many online forums providing support and a voice for victims/survivors of abuse, only a few are facilitated by qualified mental health professionals. It is in these forums that women are most likely to become aware of the nature of their abuser's damaged personality, and thereby given the means to step back and take control of their lives again. Apart from these forums, only those with access to trained mental health professionals were able to adopt this discourse (Hayes and Jeffries 2013). It is the romantic love discourse, however, that is of interest here. The following sections will explore in more depth the nature of the discourses of romantic love that keep women in their abusive relationships, and how women used those narratives to excuse their partners and accept or tolerate abuse and violence. I also examine current institutional and social support and media reporting on domestic violence and violence against women, which tends to draw on the patriarchal discourse. As we shall see, while these tend to offer explanations for violence and advice and support for disengaging, for the most part they fail miserably to over-ride the tenacious and insidious hold of the romantic love narratives for victims of abuse.

The discourse of patriarchy

In spite of much recent feminist scholarship that provides a more complex and nuanced analysis of male and female subjectivity in society (e.g. Butler 1990; Lewis and Mills 2003; McCann and Kim 2010; Wallach-Scott 2011; Negy Hesse-Biber 2012), contemporary Western-government and service-provider constructions of domestic violence draw predominately on gendered power relations, namely, the exertion of power and control by men over women (Ball and Hayes 2010; Donovan and Hester 2010). In these discourses, domestic abuse is positioned within the rather anachronous, but no less enduring notion of patriarchal power relationships that depicts the dominating social structural power of men over women. Within this framework, domestic abuse is conceptualized as a patriarchal weapon of control wielded by men to maintain their dominant position within the broader gender hierarchy. The notion of patriarchy asserts that men should dominate and control women and that domestic abuse is the individual-level expression of this broader social structural expectation (Bartholomew and Allison 2006: 102). Consequently, this discourse provides an explanation for the behaviour of male abusers.

Contemporary feminist theory provides a more refined and complex understanding of women's experience of abuse and violence, one that has been particularly instrumental in the transformation of domestic violence from an individual/private problem to a public/social issue. Nevertheless, at present in Westernized societies the earlier patriarchal discourse enjoys privilege over other discourses and is particularly evident in much of the media coverage of domestic abuse, as well as in government policies addressing the issue. Dutton and Corvo (2006: 458), for example, argue that, for over thirty years, the public policy response to the problem of [domestic violence] has been defined by activists as the socially sanctioned dominance of women by men. This view of patriarchy as the sole cause of [domestic violence] is the underpinning for a policy/practice paradigm that has dominated regulatory, legal, and policy discourse of the United States, Canada and other countries.

At the level of therapeutic intervention, this discourse is also evident in domestic violence service provision. As Seeley and Plunkett (2002: 11) note, "feminist counselling is broadly advocated as the most appropriate orientation for working with victims/survivors" because it stresses the importance of female empowerment by enabling women to make their own decisions, pointing out the power and control tactics used by men to control them. For example, the "cycle of violence" is frequently employed to illustrate the various tactics of abuse that men will use to maintain control over their female victims (e.g. Walker 1979; Smith and Seagal 2013). This approach to the problem of domestic abuse places responsibility solely with the male abuser and advocates change in men's behaviour towards and treatment of women. In other words, women are exonerated of all responsibility for the abusive relationship and the blame is shouldered by their abusers, who are acting as agents of patriarchy.

This patriarchal discourse of violence in intimate partnerships positions women as victims or survivors. The source of disempowerment is social structural, in power relations expressed through the abuse perpetrated against them by their male intimates (Seeley and Plunkett 2002: 11). For heterosexual women, at least, leaving their abusers thus presents as a somewhat insurmountable task because their individual predicament is rooted in gendered power imbalances at the broader societal level. Moreover, the problem is exacerbated by the inability of government institutions and service providers to protect women from further abuse. Most notable in this regard is the frequently reported ineffectiveness of the criminal justice system to respond appropriately to female victims of male perpetrated domestic abuse (e.g. Mugford 1989; Ptacek 1999; Epstein 1999; Crime and Misconduct Commission 2005; Douglas 2008; Douglas and Stark 2010). Thus, while the patriarchal discourse advocates female empowerment, escaping the male abuser presents as being rather overwhelming, if not impossible. How can an individual woman escape patriarchy? The therapeutic models employed within this discourse cannot answer this question because the empowerment approach is "a process of enabling [women] rather than taking a position of power by determining decisions" for them (Seeley and Plunkett 2002: 11).

The patriarchal discourse, therefore, offers little to women experiencing abuse from female partners. In spite of the recent research on abuse in same-sex relationships, which has important implications for improving policy and service provision for these women (See, e.g. Renzetti 1992 and Ristock 2002), in practice the heteronormative discourse dominates, thus failing not only to communicate directly with women in abusive relationships with other women, but also implying that abuse is not possible in female same-sex relationships (Mason 1997; Hunter 2006: 744; Hotten 2009: 13; Ball and Hayes 2010: 10). For example Merrill (1996: 11) argues that discourses of patriarchy "cannot effectively explain why domestic violence occurs in lesbian relationships because it focuses too much on socio-political aspects such as patriarchy…by observing domestic violence through gender-based analyses the existence of lesbian domestic violence is disregarded." Historically, second-wave feminism held up female same-sex relationships as the "ultimate subversion of patriarchal power and control" and by extension saw them as utopian-like, free of the power struggles and associated violence that plague heterosexual relationships (Hotten 2009: 13; Ball and Hayes 2010: 8).

Drawing on the patriarchal narrative may, therefore, lead to a lack of understanding and acknowledgement of abuse in female same-sex relationships, both for those directly involved and for society more generally. It is not surprising, then, to find that female same-sex domestic abuse is frequently misunderstood by the criminal justice system and domestic violence service providers and is therefore inadequately addressed (Giorgio 2002; Leonard et al. 2008; Hotten 2009). This suggests that attempts to engage with this discourse are unlikely to allow women to leave their abusive relationships.

In our previous analysis of online discussion forums, Sam Jeffries and I found that the patriarchal discourse was evident in both heterosexual and same-sex relationships, but was particularly challenged in discussion of the latter. Participants acknowledged their confusion over the abuse, and the inadequacy of the current discourses denying that women can abuse (Hayes and Jeffries 2013). One UK woman, for example, describes coming out as a lesbian and falling in love with a manipulative woman who isolated her from friends and family and resented her studying at university. Eventually, this partner began physically abusing the woman. Even so, the woman failed to seek help. She explains her hesitancy:

> I didn't go an [sic] see any support services because I didn't think of what was happening to me as "domestic violence". I explained it away as drugs and her abusive childhood. Part of me wanted to rescue her and it seemed very anti-feminist and wrong to blame someone for their behavior when they had come from an abusive background.

Apparently the partner had a violent and abusive childhood, having been beaten and abused by her father and brothers, and the abused woman felt that she had an obligation to help her overcome her anguish. Clearly, she is accessing scripts of romantic love, particularly the belief that one can "save" one's true love from hurt, pain and damage, and that, indeed, one has a duty to do so (Evans 2002; Power et al. 2006).

While romantic love will be discussed in more detail below, it should be noted here that most of the explanations offered by the forums' participants comprised a mixture of patriarchal, psychological and romantic love discourses. The above story, for example, highlighted the joy of coming out and falling in love, and the psychological effects of childhood abuse on her partner. However, it is the patriarchal script that prohibits blaming women that is most interesting. The same woman remarks:

> My feminist politics at the time meant that I shouldn't "blame" another woman for anything because we were all oppressed by patriarchy...

This woman describes her abusive partner as being "butch" in appearance, thereby accessing the patriarchal discourse surrounding masculinity and power – albeit female masculinity. However, her overarching identification as woman and lesbian, regardless of gender performance, seemed to stifle any attempt to associate the abuse to which she was subjected with the patriarchal scripts. Thus, the patriarchal discourse operates in a way that denies lesbian (and transgender) women their subjective experience of abuse.

Interestingly, while heterosexual forum participants drew on patriarchal understandings of abuse as men's domination over women, they were silent regarding the efficacy of these discourses, presumably taking them as a given. However, it is clear from the women's narratives in these forums that they continued to feel guilty and confused about why they stay with abusive partners. As one woman laments after a very lengthy and fairly well-informed discussion of her abuse and her understanding of it:

> Why is it that every time I think I have had enough I feel guilty about leaving? Even though my husband is emotionally abusive, I just feel terrible guilt about splitting up the family. Why can't I get past that?

She knows her husband's behaviour is abusive, but that knowledge fails to translate into action:

> I gotten [sic] just about to go so many times before and then the guilt and "what ifs" creep back in and I stay. We are currently in the honeymoon phase yet again and it makes it so hard because it makes me think that it isn't so bad but I know that it is only short lived and then it goes back to the same stuff. I am so tired of all of it and trying desperately not to give up but sometimes it seems hopeless.

Clearly, she has a good understanding of the cycle of violence drawn from earlier feminist understandings of domestic abuse. However, this seems to offer little respite other than helping to identify her partner's behaviours. She knows what is coming but feels "hopeless", and powerless to do anything about it. In the same forum, another woman has a similar story of the inevitability and hopelessness of abusive relationships:

> I'm currently "in" too, I'm having the ups and downs emotionally. As you are, we are in the "honeymoon" cycle. And you slide back thinking it wasn't all that bad, was it?! I'm trying to stay

strong...nearly impossible. The kids are fighting. I lost my cool yesterday big time. When I do, I grab my smokes and head for the garage. In all of this, I think things are good, but what about next time...you know there will be a next time and when. You'll kick yourself and remind yourself right, that's why I'm leaving. I hate the cycle, my H is unpredictable for the most part.

In contrast to the non-heterosexual women, then, the straight women are drawing on the patriarchal discourse of power and control without questioning its usefulness or relevance. Instead, they appear to be questioning themselves and their level of resolve about leaving. It appears that the patriarchal discourse is failing women. On the one hand, it disempowers lesbians and transgender women by denying them their subjective experience of abuse, while on the other, it denies heterosexual women an avenue for escape, by leaving them feeling helpless and hopeless, kicking themselves for not leaving the abusive relationship.

The discourse of romantic love

Some of the reasons most cited in the literature for women staying in or returning to abusive intimate partnerships are love, hope, feelings of commitment and loyalty to their partner (Herbert et al. 1991; Anderson et al. 2003; Karan and Keating 2007; Donovan and Hester 2010; Olson 2010). As I noted above, contemporary discourses on romantic love have no difficulty in reconciling the desire for loving, caring intimacy with violence and abuse. These discourses of romantic love are particularly powerful in Western society, especially for women, who can be forgiven for seeing as desirable the often distorted views of love depicted in films, novels and marketing hype. The discourse of romantic love, as we have already seen in Chapter 2, permeates our society and is reiterated in popular culture through film, music, television, literature, art and popular magazines. The social construction of romantic love suggests that there is a fine line between love and hate. Indeed, discursive constructions of tragic love have dominated popular culture and literature for centuries, from Shakespeare and Bronte's works, through to modern literature and culture, for example films such as *Fatal Attraction* and Stephen King's novel, *Rose Madder*. These cultural sources depict the places where love becomes enmeshed with the need to control, and demonstrate how love sometimes becomes distorted to the point where lack of ability to control love or the loved one leads to violence and abuse (Hayes and Jeffries 2013).

Although popular media scripts are overwhelmingly heteronormative, the ideal of romantic love is not specific to sexual orientation. The romantic script *is*, however, highly gendered (Power et al. 2006: 177). According to the romance script, the need to be in and subsequently maintain an intimate relationship is a uniquely feminine desire, and the nurturing nature of the stereotypical feminine ideal makes women responsible for that maintenance.

The fantasy underlying the discourse of romantic love is that it is omniscient, overwhelming and eternal (Evans 2002: 2). Consequently, narratives of romantic love idealize the fusing of identities as something fated, where love is "written in the stars", so to speak. These scripts are also informed by notions of tragedy and fate, as we saw in films such as the *Twilight* series, and also in films such as *The Time Traveller's Wife* and the Disney Princess films. Love can easily turn into tragedy where it is unrequited or damaged by infidelity, but also because it requires erotic transformation, a surrender of the self. Love is meant to be transformative. In Western romantic love scripts, the individual surrenders the self and is transformed, becoming "us" or "the couple". Love is, therefore, associated with discontinuity, disruption and disintegration of the self (Hayes and Jeffries 2013). This is particularly evident in the relationship between Bella and Edward in *Twilight*, where the already-transformed Edward becomes spiritually transformed by his desire for Bella, who in turn becomes both spiritually and (eventually) physically transformed by her love.

The disintegration of Bella's self is evident from the very beginning of the first film, where she meets and shortly becomes totally obsessed with him. Teenagers and young women alike swooned and sighed over the object of her love, clearly identifying with Bella's misdirected but clearly heartfelt need to fuse her self-identity with that of a blood-sucking vampire. In *The Time Traveller's Wife*, Henry appears out of nowhere in a field where the very young, prepubescent Clare is picnicking alone. Over the years he grooms her and she eagerly responds, declaring her love for him and her desire to be his wife before she has even reached the age of consent. When she reaches 18, Henry kisses her, and she falls completely for him, subsequently enduring a tortuous life in which he, as her husband, continues to unpredictably time-travel in and out of her life until she is forced to watch him die in agony. That someone such as Henry, who is fated to such an unpredictable and burdensome existence, would or should even choose to marry, doesn't even seem to cross anyone's mind.

It is easy to see how love may become distorted, leading to a struggle for domination and control. Popular culture and literature, both historical and contemporary, demonstrate a clear awareness of this struggle, and the inevitable pain of love. Indeed, people expect it and are resigned to it. On some level it is recognized and rejected as bad, but on another level it is regarded as just part of "being in love" – the exquisite pain of Cupid's arrow, Beyonce's "beautiful nightmare", Bronte's Heathcliff and Cathy of *Wuthering Heights*, Eminem and Rhianna's "Love The Way You Lie". Cathy ends up killing herself out of love for Heathcliff, while Rhianna openly declares her willingness to endure and even enjoy abuse and violence:

> Just gonna stand there and watch me burn?
> That's alright because I love the way it hurts.
> Just gonna stand there and hear me cry?
> That's alright because I love the way you lie...
> Love the way you lie[1]

In this sense, pain is welcomed, perhaps because it signifies the authenticity of love – because the pain of true love *is* supposed to be inevitable. A recent recording by pop songstress P!nk, titled "Just Give Me a Reason"[2] is yet another example. The song describes how her lover "stole her heart" and "fixed her", but then she discovers he's been cheating and confronts him with it. Instead of throwing him out or leaving him, she begs him to help her repair the relationship:

> Just give me a reason
> Just a little bit's enough
> Just a second we're not broken just bent
> And we can learn to love again

Heartfelt and loyal words, indeed, but in return he responds that he has no idea what she's talking about:

> I'm sorry, I don't understand where all
> of this is coming from.
> I thought that we were fine.
> Your head is running wild again
> My dear we still have everything
> And it's all in your mind.

Not only does he deny his cheating, he tells her that she is imagining things, then goes on to accuse her of not being loving enough, implying that he has an excuse to be unfaithful. Her response repeats the refrain above "Just give me a reason", as if she didn't already have reason enough to leave! As we note in our earlier research (Hayes and Jeffries 2013: 57), "these discourses clearly map out the parameters of romantic love, the expectation of pain, and the justification for pursuing the abusive relationship in spite of all the apparent negative consequences".

Given its all-encompassing and star-crossed nature, it is not surprising to find that many of the behaviours associated with expressions of romantic love are also characteristic of domestic abuse. More specifically, while possessive and controlling behaviour is abuse, the romantic discourse distorts it either as a demonstration of true love or a commitment to endurance (Wood 2001; Fraser 2005; Power et al. 2006; Karan and Keating 2007; Donovan and Hester 2011). Consequently, when one partner wants to know the whereabouts of the other every minute of the day, makes numerous phone calls to her, exhibits jealousy or discourages her from seeing her friends so that every waking moment can be spent together – this may be interpreted as an endearing demonstration of love rather than the "red flag" that it really is (Power et al. 2006: 177). Prior research conducted with both heterosexual and non-heterosexual women suggests that it can take time for "women to figure out" that these types of behaviours are not "passionate" but "scary and disabling", yet even then, the feminized discourse of romance ensures that leaving the relationship is hardly a foregone conclusion (Fraser 2005: 15).

First, this discourse associates women with acts of undying loyalty requiring them to commit to and work on maintaining their relationships even when they are abusive (Fraser 2005: 15). As noted by Power et al. (2006: 181), the discourse of romantic love prioritizes relational maintenance above all else and suggests that, "love itself can overcome all obstacles", even abuse. Thus, researchers and service providers frequently note the tendency of women to blame themselves for the abuse they experience. Women often believe that if they just try harder, love more, or be a more worthy person, then the abuse will stop because they will no longer be deserving of it (Wood 2001: 253; Fraser 2005: 17; Power et al. 2006: 181). Second, leaving abusive relationships may be difficult for women because the thought of existing outside an intimate relationship is often more painful than staying in an abusive one. This is because the discourse of romance frequently endorses the intimate relationship as the central reason for women's existence (Fraser 2005: 17). Power et al. (2006: 183) thus argues that leaving an abusive relationship can be difficult for women because "the desire to be loved, and to love romantically is pivotal to understandings of self as properly feminine subjects".

Discussion of the explicit connection between romantic love and abuse is only relatively recent, occurring primarily within the realms of academic research and scholarship. In other words, while the discourse of romantic love may be a public narrative, its connection to abuse within this space is not and, as such, women are more likely to accept distortions when they occur.

In my analysis of the online discussion forums, the pain of romantic love clearly dominated many of the threads discussing domestic abuse. There was some consensus among women participants that while love can be a glorious union between two people, the spectre of pain is always looming, is almost expected and that it is women's role to deal with it. This narrative speaks to love's perversity, and the tragedy but inevitability of the harm of romantic love. In one of the non-heterosexual forums, the following quotes were demonstrative of this:

> Why do we stay? Because we are convinced we love this person, that things will change, that it's our fault, that it will get better and that we are nothing without them.

> I look back and ask myself...why did I stay? The answer for me was a simple one....I never gave up hoping that things would change until the only thing worth saving was myself.

...you always think you can make things better. People who naturally believe in fighting for a relationship will hang in there in the genuine conviction that they can change things.

The tragedy of romantic love was also apparent in the heterosexual forums. On one thread, a woman talks about being hit, bitten and anally raped by her partner, and yet, she stayed because she loved him:

> To begin with every time he did it he apologised and said it was not his fault and that he would not do it again and blamed something like alcohol or weed. He did not apologise for the anal rapes tho [sic]. Despite this I loved him and was devastated when he instigated our break up and went right back to him for a secret relationship when he wanted to sleep with me.

Other participants are supportive and understanding of the need to fix the relationship. One woman replies:

> Doesn't any one think that people can change? And that with the right help, they will be able to get to the root of their problems and not do it again?

In another thread, a female victim who talks about her alcoholic ex-partner in similar terms, is reminiscent of Updike's poor heroine from Chapter 1:

> Shortly after falling in love with him I learned he was an alcoholic and the lies began. I tried to be patient and forgave him many things I probably shouldn't have forgiven; always hoping he maybe would appreciate it and care enough for me to stop.

This notion that love can be saved and that it is a woman's role to try harder mirrors the romantic scripts that entreat women to take responsibility for relationship success (Wood 2001: 253; Fraser 2005: 17; Power et al. 2006: 181). In many instances the fine line between love and hate is quite apparent, both on the part of the abuser and the survivor of abuse. Both heterosexual and non-heterosexual women tend to accept their abuse as part of the destiny of true love and the need to maintain love in the face of all obstacles (Hayes and Jeffries 2013). The following quote is most instructive here:

> ...I eventually came to believe I would never be anything with her, that I was useless without her, that everything was my fault and that I had to put it right to get it back to how good it had been. She cheated on me, with a man and a woman, she lied, she threatened, she abused me. And I stayed. I had to put it right. I had to give her her life back because I had messed it all up...All I had was her.

The role of woman as saviour of relationships is a clear theme across these forums (Wood 2001: 253; Fraser 2005: 17; Power et al. 2006: 181). One woman even admits that although she knows she does not have the strength to remain in a romantic relationship with her abuser, still she cannot let her go because she is certain she can help her:

> I know I don't have the strength to remain with her romantically but I do love her and I want her to get help. I think that if I really educate myself about the condition I would like to stay friends with her...If I can somehow be supportive and maintain my own sanity I would like to at least try.

The fusing of identities in the love relationship, and the willingness to be defined by it (Coleman 1994), was also evident, especially in the non-heterosexual forums, as the following story demonstrates:

> We connected in a way that I had never had with anyone else. She enchanted me and I was falling in love....After 3 months we moved in together, it seemed the right thing to do....I didn't talk to anyone except friends when we were out and I gave [her] 100% of my attention....We wanted to spend all our time together so we both quit our jobs. I thought this would be a great opportunity to prove how committed I was. We spend 24/7 together, going out all night and sleeping all day!

But this merging of two into one is the very foundation for an abusive relationship, eventually fuelling jealous and controlling behaviour in one or both partners. The creation of the romantic cocoon within which the couple is able to function as one, eventually becomes dysfunctional when inevitably exposed to the real world of work, families and other social relationships (Coleman 1994; Hayes and Jeffries 2013). The same woman continues:

> I'd lost contact with my friends, I wasn't working – and still the jealous rages continued. I was baffled.... Over the two years we spent together, my confidence with people disappeared, all my energy was spent on keeping her happy, and I desperately missed seeing my family. While we continued to have great nights out I was miserable and felt like I was continually walking on eggshells. She held my self-esteem in the palm of her hand. If she was happy, so was I, if she wasn't I tried to "fix" it. Eventually she left me for someone else – I was crushed.

Being abandoned under such circumstances results in an annihilation of the self for the victim of abuse, her very identity is so completely tied up and defined by the other, that the loss of relationship may mean a loss of what little psychological well-being the victim is able to maintain (Coleman 1994). The narrative of immersion in love, then, is possibly the most damaging discourse of all.

Conclusion

Surviving and extracting oneself from an abusive relationship appears to be a very complex issue. Not surprisingly, given the pervasiveness of the romantic love discourse in Western society, both heterosexual and non-heterosexual women seem to draw heavily on this narrative. The scripts of romantic love are implicitly and explicitly evident in both representations of abuse in popular culture and in victims'/survivors' stories. Much is made of the struggle and pain of love and relationships, of women's role in saving their relationships, the fusing of identities in love relationships and the inability of many to draw a line between making it work and tolerating outright abuse. The matter-of-fact way in which the script of romantic love was accepted without critical reflection is hugely concerning. The explicit connection between romantic love and abuse appears not to be recognized in our society; the insidiousness of Westernized notions of romantic love – that it is potentially painful, all encompassing, controlling and obsessive – is not necessarily ignored, but rather, considered an inevitable part of enduring intimate relationships. Acceptance of this discourse appears to impede women's ability to leave their abusive partners. Perhaps, as suggested by Wood (2001: 259), it is time to formulate a more healthy discourse of romantic love, or at least to gain some insight into its potential for distortion.

The script of male patriarchal power is useful for illuminating social structural reasons for men's violence against women. Not surprisingly, given the dominance of this narrative in mainstream society, women of all sexualities frequently draw on this discourse. Nevertheless, engagement with this narrative often leads to confusion. Overall, there appears to be a general sense of frustration that while having information about power and control tactics used by abusers may be enlightening, they do not provide workable strategies for leaving.

The discourse of romantic love appears to provide the strongest motivation for accepting and maintaining an abusive relationship. The patriarchal narratives are restrictive in terms of paving the way to emancipation from violent partners. However, it should be acknowledged that the foregoing research is simply observational and not necessarily generalizable. I hope it is important and useful in highlighting possible issues for more in-depth research into the role of romantic love in domestic abuse. I hope that these theoretical and pseudo-empirical musings will inform future research in a way that will impact positively on the prevalence of repeated victimization of women victims of abuse and violence.

5
Sexual Spaces

Introduction

Sex and sexuality are confusing. The amount of sexual freedom afforded adults in contemporary society is both a blessing and a curse. The resolving of this confusion is made no less urgent by the fact that sex is a gendered concept. In spite of the revolution in sexuality and gender equality over the past several decades (Bauman 2004; Weeks 2007; Halberstam 2013), women and non-heteronormative groups are still experiencing discrimination and stereotyping. If anything, women as sexual creatures have become even more governed by social discourses surrounding body and gender performance, and arguably, sexual desire (Berg 2009; Douglas 2010; Walter 2010).

This chapter explores the geography and temporality of sex and how our perceptions of sex and sexuality have developed over time. On the temporality of sex, this chapter takes from Foucault the notion that populations are governed through sex and sexuality (Foucault 1998). It draws on moments from history to illustrate how discourses have changed and what that means for contemporary sexuality. It also challenges intrinsic notions of moral harm frequently associated with sex and abuse via a critical interrogation of dominant discourses surrounding public and private spaces, and Western and non-Western spaces. This chapter draws on the theory of a geography of sex and abuse drawn from *Sex, Crime and Morality* (Hayes et al. 2012), to identify contradictions in the way we attribute good and bad sex depending on whether particular sexual interactions occur within public or private spaces, and which privilege Western sexual morality in a global context.

The geography of sex

My previous work on the geography of sex and sexuality argued that sex is governed through the legislating and policing of public and private spaces (Hayes et al. 2012). An exploration of the concepts of decency and obscenity in contemporary discourse reveals that when it comes to sex, we as a society are still fairly prudish. In spite of the emergence and exponential acceptance of the recreational sex ethic, and increased acceptability of a variety of sexualities, sex remains unequivocally relegated to the private sphere and strong sanctions apply for breaking the taboo against sex in public. Sex is a moral issue because these ways of governing are built upon assumptions about social morality – what constitutes good and bad sex and under what circumstances should sex occur – but also because sex most often is a mutual endeavour. While there were laws and religious judgements against masturbation until relatively recently, autoeroticism is now considered more or less acceptable when conducted in private. Other sexual acts, however, tend to need a partner and where people engage in mutual pursuits, the potential for mistreatment, offence or harm is always present. There is a fine line between the kind of harm that can be considered simply unethical and harm that unlawfully injures or damages someone (Hayes et al. 2012). Chapter 6 of this book will unpack some of the ways in which we can be treated unethically and immorally in sexual relations. The geography of sex, however, is based on moral judgements about the nature of sex itself. An example serves to illustrate.

On November 27, 2012 three people were arrested for disrobing in the hall outside the Speaker's office of the Capitol building in Washington DC. Brian Palmer, a journalist for Slate.com, reported that "the demonstrators were charged with lewd and indecent acts for their role in protest against proposed cuts to AIDS funding" (2012: 1). In answer to his self-posed question of why nudity should be illegal, he responds, "because it's so difficult to ignore" (2012: 1). Nudity makes us uneasy, he claims, because of its capacity to incite sexual arousal. Feinberg (1985) argues that nudity goes against the Offence Principle, which suggests that something need not in and of itself be harmful, but need only arouse an uncomfortable feeling such as shame or disgust.

The unresolved conflict between instinctual desires and cultural taboos leaves many people in a state of unstable equilibrium and a readiness to be wholly fascinated, in an ambivalent sort of way, by any sense of sexuality in their perceptual fields.

(Feinberg 1985: 17)

Public nudity is disturbing because it reminds us we are sexual beings and we have been socialized into believing that sexuality is not always under our control. This is a problem for men because the construction of masculinity requires them to always be ready for sex. Confronting nudity raises fears about losing control. Public nudity is also shameful because it is suggestive and evokes taboos that are deeply embedded in our psyches (Feinberg 1985). These taboos "speak to the perceived inability of adults to regard naked... bodies as anything but sexual" (Hayes et al. 2012: 16). The adult gaze always looks upon the body with desire. The naked body is therefore vulnerable to that desire and must be protected by clothing or privacy. The naked body is also powerful, because it has the authority to command our desire, while reminding us at the same time of our own vulnerability. But discourses around control and sexuality are also a problem for women, because women are subject to men's desire, are vulnerable in the face of it, and must therefore fear it (Hayes et al. 2012: 16). The woman's gaze must avert when confronted by male nudity because that body is a strident reminder of her vulnerability and men's potential lack of control. Even when gazing upon female nudity in the public sphere, women are forced to feel uneasy at the stark reminder of what it is about women that men desire.

Thus, public nudity, much like sexuality itself, is governed by legal moralism, grounded as it is on the belief that sex is somehow dirty or taboo, unless it is confined to private spaces (Hayes et al. 2012). The demonstrators in the example above are an affront to public decency both because they are vulnerable to the public gaze and concomitant desire, but also because they make the viewer vulnerable to his or her potential lack of control, or that of their compatriots. However, nudity is also frowned upon in private, if it is lacking consent. One cannot simply close the door and disrobe, there must be context. Children must be protected both from sex and from bodies that are suggestive of sex (Hayes and Carpenter 2012). The context for nudity is traditionally heteronormative, that is, acceptable in private spaces, between consenting adult heterosexual couples, or in some cases, for the sake of art. There are good reasons for this. The Everyday Sexism Project,[1] a social media campaign that recently attracted more than 25,000 female victims of sexual harassment, many of them victims of indecent exposure in public domains, is a case in point.

Recently, there was a flurry of activity on Twitter over a video on Upworthy.com with the headline: "If You Know Someone Who Doesn't Believe Sexism Exists, Show Them This" (Warren 2013). The video is narrated by an unnamed British woman, who it turns out is the author of the aforementioned Everyday Sexism Project. She begins by talking about how she was sexually assaulted in broad daylight in the middle of a public street: "I was just walking down the pavement one day when I suddenly felt a hand that grabbed me from behind. I was wearing jeans but pushing up between my legs... and feeling how violating that feels... just how much that sense of shame stays with you." She goes on to observe that women aren't talking about these kinds of sexual assaults and wonders why. So she decided to start a social media campaign inviting women to tell stories of being violated in public by male strangers. The response she received overwhelmed her Twitter account, with over 25,000 women tweeting their personal stories about public assaults, many of which they hadn't reported or even told anyone about. The video shows a number of women speaking about their experiences. One was assaulted on a train by a middle-aged man, who put his hand on her leg and slid it up her thigh. Another was caught in close quarters, also on a train, with a man who masturbated up against her back. When she got to work, she found semen running down the back of her skirt. The video and Twitter conversation provide clear evidence that women are being sexually harassed in a variety of situations and as a result are feeling shame and self-blame.

No woman wants to be confronted by male nudity on the train, because it is in fact the case that male nudity in this context usually does evoke desire, and, *pace* Jong's "zipless fuck", it is desire that is not invited or consented to and renders the recipient a mere object. The women reporting their experiences to the Everyday Sexism Project say they are frightened, disgusted and shamed by uninvited sexual advances and that is the crux of the matter – I suggest that women have learned to be frightened by uninvited male desire because it is the ultimate symbol of male power and control over them. "Decent" men do not engage in such activity, therefore to be confronted by a half-naked man masturbating next to you on the train is to be rendered a mere object, belittled as a receptacle of uninvited desire, and lacking power.

Contemporary women might be more open to recreational sex than ever before, they might be more willing to experiment and stretch the boundaries of the quotidian, but they want to be asked first. They also want to take their turn in exercising power, to take control and to be dominant. This is the conundrum Johnson (2002) is trying to articulate when she confronts the tensions between feminist self-empowerment and the need for passion, sensuality, commitment and, sometimes, even submissiveness. How can women empower themselves and stake their claim to equality and mutuality in sex and sexuality, when men are still succumbing to socially constructed masculinities that require them to always be ready for sex; to be expected to want sex when offered; to demonstrate sexual prowess; and, most importantly, to feel it is their due to be sexually satisfied (Connell 2005; Jensen 2007). Chapter 6 explores what happens when heteronormative masculinity and femininity become distorted, how sexual and intimate partner abuse is intricately tied to pathological extensions of the heteronormative, which is unwittingly supportive of that pathologizing. Here, though, it is most important to note the conflicting and often contradictory discourses surrounding the geography of sex.

Gendered desire

In the 1970s, when women were flying high in the wake of women's liberation, Erica Jong was one of many feminists who attempted to distil female desire and what it could mean. During this time, women began to explore and to understand that sex could be so much more than what they had previously expected. Recreational sex became the norm, even as women continued to engage in romantic partnerships and marriage (Smith 1990). The tension between free sex and romantic commitment became heightened in the 1980s, sometimes referred to as the decade of hedonism (Fletcher 2003). I have explored the development of the recreational sex ethic elsewhere (Hayes et al. 2012), but the point I want to make here is that the tension between romance and sex is not the only tension surrounding contemporary discourses on sex and intimate relationships.

Erica Jong illustrates this tension in her 1973 book, *Fear of Flying*. She describes the "zipless fuck" as the ultimate sexual freedom.

> The zipless fuck is absolutely pure. It is free of ulterior motives. There is no power game. The man is not "taking" and the woman is not "giving." No one is attempting to cuckold a husband or humiliate a wife. No one is trying to prove anything or get anything out of anyone. The zipless fuck is the purest thing there is. And it is rarer than the unicorn. And I have never had one.
>
> (Jong 2011: 14)

Jong describes her book as a "mock memoir" voiced by a "half-analyzed New York Girl in the 1970s" (Jong 2011: 4), and at the time it was one of a series of bestsellers depicting women as sexually free and experimental, that became iconic among feminists. The story follows her quest to fulfil her sexual fantasies, one of which is to experience a zipless fuck with a stranger in the darkened compartment of a train. During a trip to a conference in Vienna, she embarks on a sexual adventure that is described in erotic detail, involving her partner, and later, an affair with another man. The final leg of her journey finds her on a train from Paris to London, where she is to meet up with her partner. A young attendant enters her compartment and proceeds to pull down the window shades.

> "You are *seule*?" he asked again, flattening his palm on my belly and pushing me down toward the seat. Suddenly his hand was between my legs and he was trying to hold me down forcibly. "What are you doing?" I screamed, springing up and pushing him away. I knew very well what he was doing, but it had taken a few seconds to register.
>
> (Jong 2011: 331)

Jong's heroine finally has her fantasy come true and yet, instead of enjoying the experience, she is immediately repulsed. She screams at him to get off and runs out the door, eventually settling in another, already occupied, compartment.

It wasn't until I was settled, facing a nice little family group –
mother, daddy, baby – that it dawned on me how funny that
episode had been. My zipless fuck! My stranger on a train! Here
I'd been offered my very own fantasy. The fantasy that had riveted
me to the vibrating seat of the train for three years in Heidelberg
and instead of turning me on, it had revolted me!

(Jong 2011: 331)

Jong's heroine appears to experience the same revulsion and shame
about the incident as the women on Upworthy's video. Yet she recognizes the incongruity between her reaction and her earlier fantasy.
Upworthy's video gives us no information about the women's desires,
but we can extrapolate from the scholarly research on female sexuality that they, too, experience desire and fantasy under the right
conditions (e.g. Hite 2003; Hite 2008; Foley et al. 2012). I suggest
that while contemporary women have achieved sexual freedom and
a higher level of gender equality in terms of sexual relationships, that
freedom looks a lot different to the sexual freedom enjoyed by men.
Clearly there is a tension between sexual freedom and actual desire,
which is challenging for men and women both, especially in an age
where recreational sex is the norm.

Common folk wisdom tells us that men desire women and
women's bodies full stop, and their masculine performance of that
desire plays out opportunistically just as much as it does through
planned action. According to this view, there would be few men who
would turn down the opportunity for sex when offered by a desirable
woman, regardless of the context. Clearly, men as well as women are
buying into this norm of masculinity. Whether this is through innate
or socially constructed desire is a matter of contention, but either way
it has become the norm (Kimmel 2005). Women, on the other hand,
want sexual freedom, possibly as much as men, but they clearly perceive uninvited sexual advances as harassment (Foley et al. 2012).
The tension between women's desire and action on the one hand,
and the discrepancy between women's and men's perceptions of how
sexual desire should be acted out on the other, is one impetus for this
book. A man sees a beautiful young woman on a train and, feeling
instant attraction and desire, does not hesitate to act on it, perhaps
believing that she (or women in general) must feel the same. How
does this discrepancy between men's and women's perceptions of sex

impact on women; on men; on society in general – especially given the broad range of sexualities and forms of desire among and within genders themselves? These are some of the questions this book seeks to answer. In doing so, this chapter explores current discourses about sex as well as gender differences in perceptions of sex and intimacy. It examines the geography of sex, specifically the public and the private, and addresses the question of how perceptions of sex become distorted, leading to harassment and abuse.

Discourses on sex

The myth of great sex

Alain de Botton claims that: "Great sex, like happiness more generally, may be the precious and sublime exception" (de Botton 2012: 8). It wouldn't be unthinkable to hazard a guess that many people would agree. Yet, we are drawn into the discourse of great sex. Foucault (1998) famously argued that over the past couple of centuries, Western society has managed to make sex the very centre of our lives, in spite of all its efforts at repression. He argued that populations are governed through sex and sexuality, through the heteronormative framework of marriage, procreation and family. We have a come a long way since the 1970s and 1980s, when Foucault made his case, in terms of acceptance of non-heterosexualities and non-heteronormative ways of life, and still we are governed by discourses about great sex and perfect romance. However, while that governance continues on the one hand to focus on containing our sexuality within the normative frame of heterosexual monogamy, on the other hand we are exhorted to be free sexual beings, ready to explore and expecting nothing less than the best sex.

Johnson (2002) discusses this conundrum, noting that feminists in particular are confused about what they should expect of sex, and what should be expected of them *vis a vis* sex.

> ...while feminism may have freed women to fuck, the fuck – and "the role of the fuck in controlling women" – has in many ways stayed the same. Of equal importance, the virgin/whore divide still organizes most men's (and many women's) brains. Hence the persistence of modesty and shame closing like parentheses around supposedly liberated sex lives.
>
> (Johnson 2002: 23–24)

Johnson (2002: 25) also claims that more and more women aren't wanting sex – what she calls "the dirty little secret of a generation". She discusses a segment on *Oprah* where the women in the audience reveal just that – "they don't want it anymore". She laments that, rather than exploring the interesting underlying assumptions of that statement, Oprah chooses to frame the lack of desire as an artefact of a society in which women think of "themselves as mommies rather than hotties" (Johnson 2002: 27). The more interesting question, thinks Johnson, is what men could do to make sex more pleasurable for their partners. Laying aside the glaringly heterosexual nature of that question, could she be right? Or is it just that we have made sex such a central part of our expectations about what a good relationship is, not to mention how desirable one is, that women feel pressured to want sex – *good* sex.

Sex as recreation has created a whole new set of discourses and expectations. Sex is notoriously awkward, and our longing for sex is intricately tied to our need for physical contact in a world in which "overwhelming indifference" rules the day (de Botton 2012). "It goes without saying," quips de Botton, "that the majority of people we encounter will be not merely uninterested in having sex with us, but positively revolted by the idea" (de Botton 2012: 17). How do we reconcile that fact with the messages we are exposed to everyday in almost every sphere, telling us that being sexually desirable is the ultimate achievement and the way to hook the partner of your dreams. If you are one of the few "hotties" – and most of you who are are young or trying to stay young – then perhaps you may scoff at this claim. But if you look around at your less fortunate fellows, you will notice that most of us, while fairly okay looking, don't tend to inspire instant arousal. And yet, Johnson is arguing that even the hotties don't want sex. She cites Orenstein, who claims that, "young women...feel an entitlement to sexual pleasure on which they can't convince themselves to act" (Orenstein, cited in Johnson 2002: 26).

A male PhD student told me once that men think about sex every three minutes. According to his admittedly impressive (though uncorroborated) experience, men want sex *all the time*. According to Oprah, Johnson and Orenstein, women don't. Where is the problem located? de Botton hits the nail on the head when he remarks that

> our issues with sex are rarely about the physical act and how to improve it and make it more enjoyable...

> We worry more about how problematic sex has become with our long-term partner due to mutual resentments....Or internet porn or the fact that we only want sex with people we don't love or whether having an affair will wreck our marriage.
>
> (de Botton 2012: 8)

In short, it is social expectations about sex and love, sex and marriage, sex and relationships, or at least what we perceive as expectations, that drive us to distraction (Bauman 2004). The "loving marriage discourse", still prominent in our society (discussed in Chapter 2), collides with the great sex discourse because the likelihood of us finding one person who can cater to our every emotional, physical, procreational and sexual need for the long term is remote, and yet, we continue blindly to buy into the sex/romance/family triad. Then, when it eventually fails – as it must, given all the above – we are left blaming ourselves or feeling less than, because we failed to achieve the ideal, the prize, that is held up over all others – the perfect long-term intimate relationship with perfect sex (Johnson 2002).

A survey of social discourses online reveals that the media reinforces the myth of great sex. The "Sex and Love" sections of *Women's Health*, an online magazine whose target demographic appears to be health-conscious 20- and 30-somethings, has more than twice the number of articles on how to achieve better sex than articles about love and relationships. The opening page[2] is covered with suggestive photographs and images of couples being intimate, and headlines such as "Girl On Top" with the byline, "The best position of all time hits all the right spots. Giddyup cowgirl!" and "The Art of Aural Sex: Why do men find dirty talk so difficult?" Further down, headlines point to articles offering "35 new sex positions", "The Geography of Arousal", and "The Absolute Hottest Way to Kiss". The relationship articles, on the other hand, appear as a subdued monochromatic menu on the right side of the screen. These less-prominent headlines offer readers advice on "How To Win His Parent's Approval", and "Are You a Good Money Match?". "Relationship Fixes" and "Revive Your Romance" appear much further down the page. A similar section on sex and love on Glamour.com, a webzine with a similar age demographic, also headlines only articles about sex, followed by fashion and beauty. Relationship information again is buried in the side menu. Clearly, women are more interested in revving up their sex lives than in developing their relationships, or at least that is what the magazines are telling them they want.

An important component of the myth of great sex is the myth of frequency. Recently, an online news article in *The Independent* aroused my interest with the title "Neurotic People Need More Sex" (*The Independent* 2010). The article reported on a study undertaken by Russell and McNulty (2011) on sexual satisfaction in marriage. The study followed 72 couples over a period of four years from date of marriage and found that sexual satisfaction was not linked to frequency, except in the case of neurotics. Average frequency of sex during the first six months of marriage was once a week; by the fourth year it was three times a month. Neurotics were described as having "a tendency to experience negative emotion – neurotics get upset and irritated easily, are moody, and worry a lot". Apparently, having frequent sex makes them feel better and thereby mitigates the neurosis, creating a happier marriage (Russell and McNulty 2010: 1). The authors claim that sex has a "buffering effect" in these cases. Having sex more often improves their mood because it makes them feel desirable and raises their confidence (Russell and McNulty 2010: 1).

This study is instructive for two reasons. First, it provides the generalizable finding that most couples have sex on average around three times per month after the first year. Second, it reports that, for ordinary folk, marriage satisfaction is not based on frequency. That neurotic people feel a need to have sex more often suggests a pathological lack of self-esteem needing to be bolstered by fulfilling idealized social expectations around sex and marriage. The myth of frequency is clearly just that. While there are obviously some differences between couples, the fact that the average frequency is three times per month after four years of marriage suggests that sex is not necessarily at the forefront of the average person's mind. The belief that men think about sex *all the time* and that women are more willing than ever to engage in sexual experimentation may be tied to the general lack of availability of suitable sexual partners or perhaps to the competition for better and more attractive sexual partners. Alternatively, perhaps it is the unrealistic discourses offered by the magazines that are the driving force behind the beliefs, which in turn drive young people towards a pathological need to fulfil the social ideal. The webzines and other online sex advice columns are aimed at relatively young, unattached singles. Perhaps Russell and McNulty's findings can be explained by suggesting that when faced with constant availability, the need appears to lessen. Thus, newlyweds and young married women become the target of webzines and advice columns focusing on home, family and relationships, rather than sex, how to get it and how to do it. Again, this belies the myth that people, especially young adults, want sex as much as the magazines would have us believe.

Discourses on the sexually "deviant"

None of these discourses address sex outside of the heteronormative. Magazines and online advice columns are, as noted above, generally aimed at heterosexual men and women. Their focus on sexual prowess, seduction and desirable bodies is largely heteronormative, which is to say, traditionally stereotypical of heterosexual sex and relationships. While these discourses exhort young women to enjoy great recreational sex, they also stay fairly closely aligned with socially acceptable gender stereotypes that reinforce traditional masculinity and femininity.

A further survey of discourses aimed at non-heterosexuals reveals there is not much available, at least online. What is available is, again, confusing. As we discuss in Chapter 3, in the section on *Pathologizing Love*, discourses aimed at both gay and lesbian individuals lean towards the feminine romantic narratives. There are few, if any, sites similar to *Women's Health* and Glamour.com for gays and lesbians, and transgender individuals have even less support. The few websites and magazines aimed at same-sex relationships, samesame.com.au, for example, offer more general support, news, events and music than advice on sex. Organizations such as ACON and Healthy Communities offer referral services and information about sexual health and HIV, although they do provide pamphlets explaining gay male sex. There is very little available about lesbian or transgender sex. Most of the advice about gay and lesbian sex is posted on blogs by individuals or on gay and lesbian dating sites such as pinksofa.com, lesbianmatchmaker.com and gaydar.com. Clearly gay, lesbian, bisexual and transgender people need to go to their contemporaries to find information about sex and improving their sex life. What is clear, however, is that again, the myth of great sex is perpetuated even in non-heteronormative discourses.

The inevitable outcome of the great sex myth is twofold. First, individuals and intimate relationships that fail to live up to the myth are regarded as failures and subsequently pathologized. Secondly, the myth distorts sexuality, leading potentially to unrealistic expectations, but also to an essentializing of sexuality. This latter is particularly dangerous when individuals take on board the inevitability and instinctual nature of the sex drive, which in turn allows them to relinquish sexual responsibility and justify abusive and/or illegal sexual behaviour. These outcomes will be discussed in more detail in Chapter 6.

Surprisingly, these contradictions are even more pronounced in same-sex and other non-heteronormative relationships and sexual liaisons, though they present differently. They are also confounded by additional tensions in the geography of sexuality, which sees "deviance" governed in much the same way as sex itself, creating a situation in which those who deviate sexually from the heteronormative are doubly damned. In *Sex, Crime and Morality* (2012: 66), my co-authors and I argue that while the sexually deviant has become titillating, providing fodder for experimentation and much public discourse of a pseudo-avant-garde flavour, in fact much of this discursive activity has served to entrench and reinforce the marginalized status of non-heterosexualities:

> It has become almost *de rigeur* to be broad-minded about sex and sexuality in our twenty-first century western society. But this broadmindedness does not consist of being open to real difference at all. Rather, it employs images and ideas of "deviant" sexualities for the purposes of titillation and sexual provocation.
>
> (Hayes et al. 2012: 69)

Nevertheless, in spite of their continued status as "other" compared to their heterosexual counterparts, non-heterosexual and transgender people tend not to benefit from this apparent rise in the acceptability of sexual deviance. The titillating nature of sexual deviance sets it apart from homosexuality depending on who is involved. When women have sex with women, and men have sex with men, but do not identify as lesbian, gay or even bisexual, they receive a free ride from society on the backs of their outwardly heteronormative appearance. I do not mean just their physical appearance, which may be (and probably is) a factor, but also their personal identification as heterosexual, albeit "hetero-kinky" (Hayes et al. 2012).

Similarly, engaging in BDSM (Bondage, Domination, and Sado-Masochism) and heterosexual anal sex is relatively common (The Huffington Post 2012; Frankel 2010) – or at least the general public's taste in books, magazines, and pornographic websites suggests that it is (Media Education Foundation 2011). Thus, the spaces allocated for deviant sex are moderated by an individual's status as either hetero-kinky or "other". While the hetero-kinky are free to be relatively open about their sexuality, the Other must practice their sexuality behind closed doors or in the safe spaces and times allocated to such things – generally, Other-specific clubs, bars and bath-houses located away (or hidden) from heteronormative spaces and operated in darkness, or in the privacy of their own personal spaces and homes.

Conclusion

The geography of sex and sexuality is governed by gendered, heteronormative discourses that nevertheless draw upon and incorporate the deviant and 'othered'. Grounded in the myth of "great sex", these discourses have the paradoxical impact of allowing ostensibly greater sexual freedom than has ever before been experienced in the Western industrialized world, while at the same time creating an expectation of sexuality that is, for most people, unrealistic. Women in particular, are confused about sex, about whether to have sex and how much they should be having, and how it should make them feel. Men, on the other hand, are pressured to perform and to appear to be aggressive consumers of sex or suffer the consequences to masculinity. Both genders are subjected to traditional stereotyping, but women in particular are the focus of discrimination, particularly in the bedroom. To restate my earlier observation, women as sexual creatures have become even more governed by social discourses surrounding body and gender performance, and arguably sexual desire. Chapter 6 takes this discrimination in the bedroom as a starting point for exploring how gendered discourses of sex and sexuality lead to sexism, misogyny, and subsequently, to abuse.

6
Sexism and Misogyny

Introduction

This chapter examines contemporary constructions of masculinity and femininity and how they relate to sexual assault of women. While much progress has been made over the past decades thanks to feminist scholars' and activists' efforts to counter traditional gender stereotypes, several recent events in the UK, North America and Australia suggest that Western society is experiencing a backlash against feminism. While it has been argued that our post-modern society has moved on to become post- feminist, these recent events, among others, challenge the commonly held belief that we no longer "need" feminism. The first event involves what is called "Freshers' Week" in universities across the UK and North America. Freshers' Week is an orientation period for new students at tertiary institutions, characterized by a range of university and student-run activities aimed at making new students, who may be experiencing their first view of adult life in a new city, feel more at home.

Traditionally, there is much partying, drinking and the usual shenanigans alongside the more formally organized events on campus. However, on September 20, 2013, Laura Bates reported in *The Guardian* a rather disturbing trend in this year's festivities. The article, entitled "Freshers' week sexism, and the damage it does", reports a range of "laddish" behaviour that clearly not only is sexist, but which speaks to an underlying rape culture. She writes,

> This week, a special council at St. Mary's University in Canada is reviewing orientation activities carried out at the university, after

a video was posted online showing 80 student leaders celebrating the first week of the university term. They were chanting (in front of new first-year students): "Y is for 'Your sister', O is for 'Oh so tight', U is for 'underage', N is for 'No consent', G is for 'Grab that ass'." The story came just weeks after a poster advertising a fresher's week event at Cardiff Metropolitan University prominently featured a picture of a T-shirt bearing the words: "I was raping a woman last night and she cried."

(Bates 2013)

Bates claims that the whole sexist tone of Freshers' Week began more "subtly" some weeks earlier with an emailed article to prospective students at UCAS describing university housemates as "mum figures" and "dad figures" taking on traditional gender roles. As students began to arrive on campus, many more incidents were reported. *The Guardian* asked students on Twitter to "share their experiences of #FreshersWeekSexism" and according to Bates, "the responses came thick and fast", via the @EverydaySexism project:

Halls rep to a fresher: "I'm going to treat you like a dolphin, segregate you from the group until you give into me". @EverydaySexism

@EverydaySexism A classmate laughed when I said I wanted to play football for the Uni team, assuming that women can't play football.

@EverydaySexism Someone on my facebook had just used the phrase "It's not rape if it's freshers" #FreshersWeekSexism luckily not at my uni.

(Bates 2013)

Phrases such as "fresher fishing" describe the rash of blatant harassment aimed at young women during this week, including one female student "being pinned against a railing against her will", while others reported "being grabbed, touched and harassed". Bates points out that such behaviour sends young women "the message, loud and clear, that they are seen as sexual prey, and that their bodies [are] public property". These reports follow hot on the tail of a report of student activity at Yale University in the USA, where Delta Kappa

Epsilon students recently marched across campus chanting, "'No' means yes, 'Yes' means anal; 'No' means yes, 'Yes' means anal..." (Keith 2012). Clearly, universities are being overtaken by what has, in the UK, been termed "laddish culture", and in the USA, "bro culture" (Keith 2012), both characterized by contempt for the feminine, while at the same time, a desire to exploit it.

Some months prior to this, across the other side of the world in Australia, another form of sexism had reared its ugly head. Former Labor Prime Minister, Julia Gillard, was accused of playing "the gender card" in politics – a phrase the Liberal National Party (LNP) and other Labor opponents often used to immediately discount and render invisible any point about gender equality that a woman (especially a woman in any kind of leadership role) might be trying to make (Goldsworthy 2013). In October the previous year (2012), Gillard was accused in Parliament by Tony Abbott, then Leader of the Opposition, of being sexist and misogynist because she continued to support a Labor MP who had been accused of sending sexist text messages. Abbott and his party had called for the offender, Peter Slipper, who was also Speaker, to stand down or be sacked, but Gillard stood by him (Jones 2012). In response to Abbott's accusation, Gillard gave a stirring speech to Parliament – now known as "The Misogyny Speech"[1] – that went viral on YouTube. The world applauded her, while at the same time she was being derided for "playing the gender card" by her own compatriots (Goldsworthy 2013).

When Gillard formed a "Women for Gillard" group in the lead up to the 2013 federal election, she was once again silenced, this time by the media. Just prior to this, the LNP had hosted a dinner at which the restaurant owner had distributed a menu describing one of the dishes as "Julia Gillard Kentucky Fried Quail – Small Breasts, Huge Thighs and a Big Red Box" (Overington 2013). Gillard commented that the menu showed a "lack of respect" and left it at that. Nevertheless, an unnamed journalist for *The Australian* commenting on "Women for Gillard" reported that "yet again, Julia Gillard has played the gender card to distract voters from Labor's policy challenges and the continuing speculation about her leadership, and to set up a phony dichotomy with Tony Abbott" (*The Australian* 2013). The article goes on to belittle Gillard for "describ[ing] the election as 'a decision about whether, once again, we banish women's voices from our political life'." This was a clear misrepresentation of Gillard's overall platform, which was to include women's voices, but not as her only, or even her major aim. These deliberate misrepresentations of the first female Prime Minister of Australia, the accusations of misogyny, and of playing the gender card, the endless comments about her attire and desirability or otherwise of her various body parts, the tawdry jokes about her sexuality and her relationship with her partner, and the jibes about her private hobbies (such as knitting), all served to disparage the leader of a nation that prides itself on "the fair go" (Goldsworthy 2013). They also reveal a disturbing trend towards misogyny, not only in politics, but in everyday life.

This chapter explores and unpacks this trend, and argues that it is part of a larger backlash against feminism that is dogging not only Commonwealth countries, but Western nations as a whole. Feminists have already documented the backlash against feminism and girl-power that occurred in the 1990s (Faludi 1991). That backlash was characterized by a return to hegemonic masculine values and behaviours, especially among the working class. This new millennium backlash, however, presents in a variety of different ways – in laddish, "bro" and "blokey" culture not necessarily attached to working-class men; in everyday sexism against women fuelled by social media; in the ever diminishing size of women's bodies and the amount of space they are allowed to occupy; and most importantly, in the diminishing of women's voices and action against sexual assault and harassment.

Bodies and moral spaces

Women's ideal bodies have been shrinking for decades, and they have been doing so deliberately. Where several decades ago the average female model was a size 12, today she is a size 2. Women's sizing is beginning to mimic baby clothes, with the recent introduction of size zero and even double-zero. "Nothing tastes as good as skinny feels," boasts supermodel Kate Moss (Wardrop 2009), who is herself a super-skinny size zero. Lovett (2012) reports that in North America,

> [m]ost runway models meet the body mass index criteria for anorexia, according to an editorial pictorial in the January issue of PLUS Model magazine.

Twenty years ago, the average fashion model weighed 8 percent less than the average woman. Today, she weighs 23 percent less, it said. When asked for its source, the magazine cited the website of Rader Programs, which treats those with eating disorders.

Plus-size models have shrunk, too. A decade ago, plus-size models averaged between size 12 and size 18. Today, the majority of plus-size models on agency boards are between size 6 and size 14, the magazine said, based on its own research.

While the average North American woman weighs 23 per cent more than these models, it is not for lack of trying. Lovett (2012) reports that half of women surveyed by Plus Magazine are a size 14 or larger. Standard sizes in both major stores and boutiques, however, are size 14 and below. In Australia, Warrington (2013) reports that a survey of 1,300 women aged 18–100 revealed the average Australian woman is a size 16 (US 12). A 2000 survey commissioned by British Corporation Marks and Spencer found that the average dress size had increased from a (UK) 12 to a 14 in the previous decade (Mullins 2000). By 2008, it had increased to a size 16 (Salter 2008). It is for this reason that UK department store, Debenhams, recently announced that it would be introducing size 16 mannequins to more accurately reflect British women.

This move has yet to be adopted in Australia, however. There appears to be no continuity whatsoever in women's sizing in Australian retail outlets (Angel 2013). My own experience reflects this, as my wardrobe currently contains wearable clothing from size 10 through 16. Some stores and manufacturers deliberately cater to smaller women, especially those targeting teens and pre-teens. However, many of the more popular semi-upmarket outlets are deliberately making their sizes larger. Clothing labels Cue and Veronica Maine, for example, tend to run their garments at a size larger than stated on the label, perhaps catering to the egos of those women with incomes generous enough to afford them. Nevertheless, it is still difficult for a "plus size" (read, size 16 and above) woman to buy clothing off the rack because larger sizes are merely proportionally expanded versions of sizes 8 and 10, making them ill-fitting for many women whose weight may be distributed unevenly. Indeed, the University of Adelaide's National Size and Shape Survey (Henneberg 2002) reported that at least 50 per cent of women "can't find clothes to fit" (Sharp Dummies 2013).

Many women are therefore literally forced into exercise and diet regimes, or into wearing ridiculously constricting corsets and girdles aimed at shrinking their circumference to an acceptable size and shape. I don't think it necessary here to rehearse the statistics surrounding the enormous size and pervasiveness of the weight loss industry. There is evidence enough in every supermarket, pharmacy, health food store and fitness club with which we come into contact on a daily basis, not to mention the ocean of advertisements for these products and services in magazines, online, on television and the backs of buses. The question being begged is not whether this signals an "obesity epidemic" as we are so often told, or even why women are getting bigger. The question is why are they being named and blamed for their size, and made to feel as if their inability to maintain a size 2 is a personal and collective moral failing.

Oliver (2006: 1) argues that concern about the so-called "obesity epidemic" is "fueled more by social prejudice, bureaucratic politics, and industry profit than by scientific fact". It makes political sense to blame people for being overweight, and to shame them into buying into weight loss regimes, but it does not make common sense at all to personally blame an entire group of people for becoming the product of their times. More sedentary work, computers, technology, outsourcing and more sedentary pastimes have become the norm, while television ads and food programs relentlessly peddle more and more high-calorie, delicious-looking food (Oliver 2006). Of course, this affects men as well as women, but it is women who bear the brunt of moral failure, not men. Men's attire is simple compared to women's, and it is a very large man indeed who must shop in a specialty store, a far cry from over half of women who cannot find clothes to fit, women who aren't necessarily obese or dangerously overweight – they are the "average women" in our society (Sharp Dummies 2013).

Meanwhile, even women who can find clothes to fit are inundated with advertisements and marketing campaigns that tell them they need to be much thinner. This disjunction between women's actual sizes and the socially constructed ideals of feminine beauty and health reflect a gendered geography of bodies that dictates the amount of space women and men are entitled to occupy. In her poem, "Shrinking Women", Lily Myers explains with remarkable insight how women have been taught to "create space around" themselves, to create more "space for the entrance of men into their lives". She ponders on how her mother seems to shrink in size each time she visits, how she measures everything she eats and how at night she hears her creep into the kitchen

> to eat plain yoghurt, in the dark, a fugitive stealing calories to which she does not feel entitled. Deciding how many bites is too many.
>
> How much space she deserves to occupy.
>
> (Myers 2013)

She goes on to ponder how this legacy of shrinking women in her family has affected her.

> I have been taught accommodation
> My brother never thinks before he speaks.
> I have been taught to filter.
> "How can anyone have a relationship to food?"
> He asks, laughing, as I eat the black bean soup
> I chose for its lack of carbs.
>
> (Myers 2013)

That men "grow out" and women are taught to confine themselves is no less true for the 50 per cent of women who can't find clothes to fit. I would argue that women are not given permission to freely take up space, to spread out and be comfortable. Restricted by fashion, by underwear, but also by social prejudice that threatens to frown should they dare eat anything remotely palatable, women are forced to "steal calories in secret" because they do not feel entitled. As a reinforcement of this militaristic governing of their bodies and spaces, women gain increased significance and value the less space they inhabit, especially if they accompany their diminutive status with appropriate decoration, in most cases, the skimpier the better. The crowning achievement, however, is a diminutive frame with big breasts, a condition that is completely unnatural except for a very, very small number of women – most of whom are Victoria's Secret models. Thus, even for naturally slim women, the pressure to become big-breasted is pervasive. Cue the vast cosmetic surgery industry and we also have a medical imperative for pursuing the ideal female body. This gendered geography of bodies is moral in nature because it makes individuals responsible for fitting into a social ideal, and blames and denigrates them when they do not. It is therefore also distinctly sexist and arguably misogynistic, first because it discriminates against women, but also because the shrinking and diminishing of the ideal of female beauty and health speaks to a distaste for and even disgust of women who are fleshy, round, ample, soft, and fecund. Such women are undesirable because they are non-conforming. Appliance corporation LG's recent advertising of a vacuum cleaner is instructive here. The LG Kompressor Plus vacuum cleaner is seen sucking onto the back of a bikini model who is being photographed in various seductive poses. When the photographer calls it a wrap, the vacuum cleaner is turned off and as it detaches from the model's back, we see her body quickly "inflate" into an obese shape – the vacuum having presumably been used to literally suck away her fat. The video clip of the ad went viral on YouTube,[2] and when people (usually women) commented on its bad taste in the way it makes fun of big women, the reply was usually along the lines of "get a sense of humour". A post by "Jennifer" on about-face.org, a blog dedicated to challenging stereotypes, commented on this ad that:

> It is the Trojan Horse of themes. Society is informed enough to know that the portrayal is tongue in cheek... [but] Beneath it, we are still buying into the stereotype that thin is acceptable and desirable and other body weights must be demonized, contained, and "sucked" away.
>
> (about-face.org 2012)

The obese woman in the ad is humorous because she is the exact opposite to what we were expecting – the thin, beautiful, blonde model in the red bikini becomes the size 20 freak who dares to so literally take up three times as much space. She is not considered pretty or attractive in any way, let alone capable of modelling bikinis.

Admiration and desire are the sole reserve of she who is able to take up as little space as possible, who accommodates our expectations about desirability and beauty, and who makes herself conformably decorative. The extreme of this trend can be seen in the current fashion for waist-cinching and "waist-training" corsets, aimed at training the body to be nipped in at an ungainly and dangerous proportion to the rest of one's body, allowing even the thinnest women to become even more emaciated in the name of fashion. A 24-year-old German woman, Michele Kobke, recently gained reknown for wearing one such corset day and night for three years to reduce her waist from 25 to 16 inches (Styles and McCann 2013). Apparently she was inspired by the current Guinness world-record holder for the smallest waist on a living woman, 70-year-old Cathie Jung, whose waist is 15 inches. Kobke's goal is to make her own waist small enough to take the world record, in spite of reporting that she can now barely stand or keep herself upright without the corset, has trouble breathing because her lungs are constricted and has to eat many very small meals per day to accommodate her squashed digestive system (Styles and McCann 2013).

I venture to suggest that this sad behaviour is a form of internalized misogyny. Says Kobke: "It embraces me and gives me [a] pretty, defined waist. It feels nice and smooth. It's unique ...My life hasn't changed, just slowed down a little...Now my movement is more feminine" (cited in Styles and McCann 2013). Her desperate need to be noticed, paradoxically by making herself smaller, reflects at the very least a clear dislike of her body and a frightening willingness to deliberately disfigure herself so she can look and act more feminine. One is reminded of the breathless heroines of Victorian novels who were constantly swooning for being similarly laced-in and confined to restrictive but highly ornamental attire. Apparently, two centuries of progress in both fashion and gender equality have done little to dampen women's desire to assume the role of the lithe, breathless heroine in need of rescue.

Laddism and the disease model of feminism

There is an infamous and much-critiqued article in the November 2003 issue of *Maxim*, titled "How to Cure a Feminist" (*Maxim* 2003: 58). The full-page article outlines four stages of "treatment", with photographs to illustrate. The images are of the same woman, transformed from the first stage in which she is depicted wearing jeans and a tank top (the proverbial "wife beater") with messy hair and a cigarette hanging out of her mouth, to the fourth stage, in which she is saucily posed, heavily made-up and dressed in see-through underwear, at which she is teasingly tugging. Stage two shows her neatly dressed, hair combed, and smiling, while stage three depicts her posing in little-girl style with pigtails and a finger hooked coyly in her mouth. Each image has a speech bubble attached to the model's head. Stage 1 says, "There'd be no more wars if all penises were cut off! Argh!"; stage 2, "Maybe you're not a bum like my absentee father"; stage 3, "I think a man completes me"; and finally, stage 4 says, "Your Camaro makes me so hot". This last image is over-stamped with the word "CURED".

The disease model of feminism is not confined to magazines such as *Maxim*, but is a fundamental building block – perhaps even the foundation itself – of "lad" and "bro" culture in contemporary Western society. Lad culture, or laddism, endorses and celebrates stereotypically anachronistic masculine values such as physical and sexual prowess, binge drinking and homosocial bonding. According to Nylnd (2007: 9), Lad culture derives from

> ...the postmodern transformation of masculinity...the 1990s "new lad" was a clear reaction to the "new man"...most clearly embodied in current men's magazines, such as *Maxim*, *FHM* and *Loaded*, and marked by a return to hegemonic masculine values of sexism [&] male homosociality.

Faludi (2000: 594) claims that, at that time, "men saw themselves as battered by feminism". Weldon (2012: 61) concurs, arguing that, "laddishness is a response to humiliation and indignity...the *Girl-Power! Girl-Power!* female triumphalism which echoes through the land".

While there is recent scholarly research demonstrating a shift in the other direction towards a softened and inclusive masculinity, especially among younger men (Anderson 2011), it is unclear whether these two opposing cultures – inclusive masculinity and laddism – are class-based, or whether there is some other factor or factors involved. In both the UK and North America, bro-culture appears to be rife on university campuses, as we saw in the introduction to this chapter. In Australia, it resides on campus to some extent, but is mostly constrained in the public sphere to social media sites outside the university. This means that it is not necessarily young working-class men involved, although universities in these countries have all recently instituted policies to increase accessibility by low socio-economic groups. The sexist and misogynist behaviour extends to top-tier campuses such as Yale and Oxford, which are disproportionally populated by the more privileged classes (Keith 2012). The backlash against the disease of feminism, then, is widespread among young men in those countries. The goal of eradicating any pretentions to gender equality is high on their agenda.

It should be noted, as was also mentioned in the introduction to this chapter, that misogyny and sexism are not peculiar to Generation Y. It resides, I would argue, in the very fabric of Western society as a whole. Nevertheless, it is worth exploring the phenomenon of lad and bro culture in some depth in order to uncover the rationale behind the backlash against feminism.

In his documentary film, "The Bro Code", Keith (2012) hypothesizes four stages in the "training" of the contemporary sexist male: (1) "Train men to womanize"; (2) "Immerse them in porn"; (3) "Make rape jokes"; and (4) "Call in the masculinity cops". The film offers searing examples of each stage, drawing on everything from popular culture to actual interviews with young men to document the social impact of bro culture. In particular, he cites "bros before hoes", a phrase popular on North American university campuses, and suggests that their world is divided into two kinds of men: "the Maxim man" and the klutz/dork/nerd (Keith 2012). On campus, one is either a bro or a hopeless klutz. The homosocial loyalty to one's bros, and the labelling of women as whores (hoes) creates a culture in which young men are able to dominate and control women. Women must be hot, and they must be "ready for it" (sex), an attitude that is bolstered and reinforced by Hip Hop and rap artists such as 50 Cent and Eminem, and films such as "Magnolia", in which Frank T. J. Mackey (played by Tom Cruise) gives his famous "Respect the cock" speech, the clip of which has also gone viral on YouTube[3]:

> Respect the cock!...And tame the cunt! Tame it! Take it on head-first with the skills that I will teach you at work and say no! You will not control me! No! You will not take my soul! No! You will

not win this game! . . . . You are embedding this thought. *I am the one who's in charge. I am the one who says yes! . . . No! . . . Now! . . . Here! . . .*

(IMDB nd. My emphasis)

Women will be dominated because "we are men!" But also because, in the immortal words of 50 Cent,

> Ooh, she wants it, uh uh, she wants it
> Ooh, she wants it, uh uh
> (So)
> I got to give it to her[4]

In bro culture, women are (or should be) willing objects of control and domination, desperate for a "real man" to "give her what she wants". Women are also body parts – they are breasts, legs, arses, and lips. In the *Maxim* article described above, the masculine-looking feminist is turned into a simpering, almost naked model – "an actual woman". An actual women is presumably one who is stereotypically feminine, submissive, and ready for sex at any time. *Maxim*'s "2013 Hot 100: The Definitive List of the World's Most Beautiful Women" is available on their website (at time of writing) and also as a separate publication on their iPad App, Maxim+, which supports subscription to the tablet version of *Maxim*. Out of the 100 women photographed for this special issue, only eight are pictured fully clothed (that is, with no body parts revealed). Surprisingly, one is actress Megan Fox, who is described as "Queen of the MILFs".[5] Presumably her demure attire is a concession to her status as a mother. California Attorney General, Kamala Harris (number 54), is also dressed conservatively in a suit, accompanied by the comment: "President Obama might have had to apologize for calling this California girl 'the best looking attorney-general in the country', but we will do no such thing." The majority of women in this spread are dressed in scant swimwear, skimpy underwear, or are naked. At number 41, Malin Akerman stands with a toy long-nosed pistol across her chest, a flag marked "Bang" hanging from its barrel – a classic symbolic association of sex with violence if ever there was one. Apart from Harris and Fox, the rest of the women are posed seductively, typically looking into the distance, or eyes cast down, lips open, hands holding or stroking some part of themselves, or with a finger in their mouth, ready to be touched and held, submissive, waiting. Bodies are twisted provocatively to display breasts and crotch, and there is much hair blowing in the breeze.

At number 1, Miley Cyrus is quoted as saying, "It's every woman's fantasy to be told she's No.1 on *Maxim*'s Hot 100! So Crazy!" Interestingly, it is a picture of her back that we first see of her. She is leaning against a wall, arms spread out, head tilted slightly to the side, wearing only a pair of old jeans ripped across one buttock to reveal no underwear beneath. She also wears a gold necklace that looks like a collar and leash hanging down her back. Cyrus's pose mimics a prisoner (or a lover?) tied up by the arms, ready for a lashing. The tear across her bottom suggests the lashing has already started. The overall image speaks of submission, passivity, waiting and an expectation of (more) violence.

The clincher in the *Maxim* spread, however, is number 69, cutely titled "Manti Te'o's Fake Girlfriend". The reference refers to Notre Dame linebacker (at the time), Manti Te'o, who was mocked by media and fans alike in 2012 for allegedly fabricating a girlfriend he called Lennay Kekua. Both Te'o and his manager claimed that he was the victim of a hoax, but the story nevertheless went viral. The photograph in *Maxim* shows a tiny black bikini suspended in midair apparently upon an invisible woman, where all we see is the molded swimsuit against a tropical island beach backdrop. The caption states, "One of the year's most talked about women was invisible and had the voice of a dude. How can you not fall under her charming spell?" While it is not difficult to appreciate the humour in *Maxim* including the hoax woman in the Top 100, the caption is both shocking and disturbing. That no man could resist a woman who is invisible and sounds like a man sums up the misogynistic undercurrent typical of the bro code. Women are for sex, they are objects without identities and as such need not be acknowledged as subjects of their own fates or owners of their own bodies. They will fit the mold of what a "hot" woman must look like, and they must be available, submissive, and with no voice to interrupt or ask for anything. The fact that she is both invisible and has a man's voice speaks to the homosocial loyalty of men to each other, where women's voices are eradicated altogether, leaving only eroticized parts of their bodies to be desired or used at whim. The violent hatred of feminists typical of bro culture is directed at any woman daring to actually have a voice, to demand that they own their own bodies, and that they deserve space in the world apart from the spaces they occupy as objects.

And in case men forget the bro code, the "masculinity cops" are everywhere. In the USA, an ad for Miller Lite beer shows three men at a bar. When one walks up, his friend says "That's not a Miller Lite!" The scene continues:

> *Bro 1*: "Light beer's light beer!"
> *Bro 2*: "No, Miller Lite has more taste."
> *Bro 3*: "Strike 2!" (holds up two fingers) "One more, I'm taking your man card."
> *Bro 1*: "My man card?! What was strike 1?"
> (the shot crosses to an earlier scene where they are playing pool)
> *Bro 1*: "Hey B, I'm goin to the bathroom. You comin?"
> *Bro 3*: "What?!" (Bro three and women with him all look disgusted)
> *Bro 1*: "Come on..!"
> (Shot cuts back to original scene in which Bro 1 hangs his head in shame.)
> *Bro 1*: "You're right"
> *Voice Over*: "Man up and choose a light beer with more taste!"[6]

This ad packs a double whammy because it is sexist against both men and women. Bro 1 is denigrated for engaging in the stereotypical female behaviour of asking a friend to accompany him to the bathroom. Even the women in the ad make fun of Bro 1, suggesting that real bros do not engage in such "girly" behaviours. Both men and women in this ad pose as masculinity cops, policing male behaviour to ensure that the bro code is not broken. The threat of losing one's "man card" appears to be the worst possible punishment for these men, and the same could be said of men in general. The policing of masculinity ensures that men are reminded of the "rules of manhood" at all times, and to give out "verbal and behavioural citations" when necessary to tow the offender back into line (Keith 2012). A convenient side effect of masculinity policing is that it reinforces negative stereotypes of femininity and womanhood, while at the same time denigrating them and therefore women in general.

Internalized sexism

Not only are women silenced and invisible, they must also compete with each other. Pseudo-reality television shows such as *Jersey Shore* and *Geordie Shores* depict traditional sexist values where men strut and expect women to compete for their attention. In one episode of *Jersey Shore*, for example, male character Ronnie says,

> I got three words: beers, bitches and the beach. That's all you need to know about the Jersey Shore. I mean, I don't really know what love means. You just take your shirt off and they come to you. It's like a fly comes to shit.
>
> (Media Education Foundation 2011: 3)

Judging from women's responses on these and other shows, many of them appear to have taken their assumed role to heart. It is not uncommon to hear young women routinely refer to each other as bitches – where "yo, bitches!" is a term of endearment just as often as a symbol of enmity. Women call each other, and allow men to call them animals, as if it means raunchy, when in reality, men's use of the term "bitches" reflects a deep contempt for women. It also reflects women's contempt for themselves. On *Geordie Shores*, which satirical writer Natasha Warren (2013) calls "The Big Mac of the junk TV world", a group of young people is taken out of Yorkshire in the UK and deposited onto a tropical resort, they spend hours on getting ready to go out to clubs where they hope to meet a hot guy and have sex with him. Their appearances mimic the Top 100 models on *Maxim's* list with their skimpy dresses that allow a generous showing of cleavage, midriff and thigh, stiletto shoes, heavy makeup and long, carefully styled and sprayed hair. At the club they vie with each other, and talk behind each others' backs. Popular singer Chelley sums it up nicely in the following lyrics:

> Hate hate hate hate hate
> I don't care what these chicks say
> I don't even look their way
> Look their way look their way
> Every time I walk in the club
> They hating on me cuz they know I look good

> My hair done right and my dress real tight
> All eyes on me I took the night.[7]

Divide and conquer is a popular theme in lad and bro culture, and it is especially successful when women begin to see each other as rivals. In hating each other, they admit their acceptance of sexism. Erotic competition and battle is evidence that this sexism has been internalized and has become self-regulating. Lad culture's mission is accomplished.

The flip side of lad culture and the competition for men is the evolution of what has been termed the "ladette", a subculture of young women whose sole aim is to beat men at their own game. These women mimic men's roles as a way of regaining control (Keith 2012), and are best personified by celebrities such as Ke$ha, and J-Woww from *Jersey Shore*. Says J-Woww in one episode:

> If you don't know me, then you hate me, and you wish you were me. I am like a praying mantis, after I have sex with a guy I will rip their heads off. Let the party begin bitch. Because I have a bad habit of playing little emotional games with men. When they date me, it's cool in the beginning, we do our thing in the first month, and then I send them on a roller coaster ride to hell.
>
> (Cited in Media Education Foundation 2011: 9)

Make no mistake, this "beating him at his own game" tactic appears empowering, but in reality it is just another form of internalized misogyny. Ke$ha tells a man to "zip his lip" and "Don't be a little bitch with your chit chat; Just show me where your dick's at" in her raunchy song titled "Blah, Blah, Blah", but on another hit single, she laments her addiction to a man who makes her unhappy.

> What you got, boy, is hard to find
> I think about it all the time
> I'm all strung out, my heart is fried
> I just can't get you off my mind!
> Because your love, your love, your love is my drug[8]

Clearly, the raunchy ladette persona is incapable of sticking for very long – testament, possibly, to the fact that such "masculine" behaviour is not so ingrained in ladettes as it is in lads.

Pornography and abuse

In *The Bro Code*, Keith's second condition for training men to be sexist is to "immerse them in porn". Again, I do not want to rehearse the usual debates over whether pornography is sexist and misogynist. Rather, this section moves straight past "traditional" pornography (that is, pornography that is more or less strictly erotic, where women may appear submissive, but in which there is no physical violence or non-consensual sex) to discuss a genre of porn referred to as Gonzo, and the notion of the "hate fuck". Keith (cited in Media Education Foundation 2011: 12) describes the former thus:

> Known for its more humiliating and violent form of pornography, Gonzo has become a sort of sexual *Jackass*, for a generation of boys who are attracted to seeing women degraded and abused. Take one part hard core sex, one part abuse to women, and you have Gonzo porn.

According to Keith, Gonzo is one of the most downloaded forms of pornography in the USA today, which suggests that "degrading women is incredibly attractive to many men", a horrifying thought. To get an idea of the volume of material we are talking about, Keith (cited in Media Education Foundation 2011: 10) claims that "the porn industry makes more profit than Microsoft, Google, Amazon, Ebay, Yahoo, Apple and Netfliz combined". Ex-porn addict and author of five books on pornography, Michael Leahy, claims to have conducted a survey of 25,000 university students, the results of which revealed that the average age at which boys are first accessing pornography on the internet is 12–13, while for girls it is age 16 plus (Leahy 2008). So the fact that Gonzo is the most popular genre of pornography suggests that the kind of sexual education pubescent and teen boys are accessing is not one that applies very well to real life. Dines (2010) argues that while many boys and men initially find Gonzo abhorrent, substantial exposure to regular porn increases their threshold for abuse and violence because they become bored. Pornography – even Gonzo – is so formulaic, she claims, that men often feel the need to "up the ante", becoming more and more desensitized until eventually they "cross the line" into abusive material (Dines 2010). In her research on the impact of pornography (specifically Gonzo) on sexuality, Dines visited hundreds of such sites, one of which is called "Gag Me Then Fuck Me". The opening words on the site read:

> Do you know what we say to things like romance and foreplay? We say fuck off! This is not another site with half-erect weenies trying to impress bold sluts. We take gorgeous young bitches and do what every man would really like to do. We make them gag til their makeup starts running, and then they get all their other holes sore – vaginal, anal, double penetrations, anything brutal involving a cock and an orifice.
>
> (cited in Dines 2010, Loc 176)

She reports that a study conducted on the content of contemporary pornography sites found that almost all of the 50 most rented movies were filled with many scenes of physical and verbal abuse of women (Wosnitzer and Bridges 2007, cited in Dines 2010). Acts of physical aggression included slapping and gagging, while verbal abuse included calling the women slut and bitch. Much like *Jersey Shore* and 50 Cent music videos, these movies and websites reinforce the notion that women are objects for male use (Media Education Foundation 2011: 10). According to Keith (cited in Media Education Foundation 2011: 13), "hate porn" has become mainstream, as has the term "hate fuck". JM Productions Videos, which produces videos in which a man has sex with a woman and then flushes her head in a toilet, is cited by both Dines (2010) and Keith (2011) as a prime example of hate porn.

> The production company states, and these are their very words, "Every whore gets the swirlies treatment. Fuck her, then flush her."
>
> (Keith, cited in Media Education Foundation 2011: 13)

The fact that men want to hate fuck a woman is concerning, to put it mildly. It dehumanizes women and potentially opens them up to danger, not only in the porn films themselves, but in real life. This is not to suggest that men cannot tell the difference between film and real life; rather, it creates a pathway for thinking about women as objects of hate and scorn, and while the majority of men would never act on such beliefs and attitudes, it certainly paves the way for those few who would. But more alarmingly, the sheer availability of such material and the rabid consumption of it by men, sets women up to more deeply internalize the misogyny.

Fed on a diet of novels such as the *Fifty Shades of Grey* series,[9] arguably a prime example of how abuse in relationships can be portrayed as consensual BDSM (Barker 2013), women have been primed to think that being bitten and slapped around a bit is sexy and acceptable. While the books portray the sexual activities between protagonists Anastasia and Christian as consensual, their relationship as a whole is startlingly heteronormative and conservative, with Christian playing the dominant and experienced lover and Ana the young, submissive and accepting virgin. Indeed, Dymock (2013: 880) argues that the mass appeal of *Fifty Shades* promotes "the production of sexual identity as commodity", that it

> demonstrates that, rather than a politically progressive utopian strategy that might delimit the parameters of sexual desire, transgression now primarily functions as a mechanism through which capitalism is reinforced and the institutions of heteronormativity maintained.

Porn tells men that no really means yes; *Fifty Shades* tells women the same thing, though in the form of consensual non-consent. The *Twilight* series also depict the heroine as begging to be crushed, potentially gored, and even killed by her would-be lover. The result for women can only be confusion at the very least over where to draw the line in sex play, and at the very worst, in the kind of internalized misogyny that leads women to stay in sexually, physically, emotionally and verbally abusive relationships. The fact that *Twilight*, *Fifty Shades of Grey* and *The Time Traveller's Wife* were all written by women over the past decade is even more telling. These smart, arguably talented and extremely successful female authors are positioned as authoritative, and are, perhaps, even more influential as role models than the heroines and plotlines of their novels.[10]

Sexism and sexual assault

American research clearly demonstrates that young women, particularly those on American university campuses and those who live and work in urban areas, are more likely to be sexually assaulted than any other group (Carr and Van Deusen 2004; Media Education Foundation 2011). It is unclear whether this is also the case in Australia, Europe and other Western nations. However, recent news and media reports from Canada and the UK highlight the dangers of sexual assault for women on campus (Kingston 2013; Dehaas 2013; The Canadian Press 2013; Royal College of Psychiatrists 2011). In spite of these reports, and the statistics about rape and assault among women in general, rape jokes continue to flourish on television and in popular culture, young men continue to turn a blind eye to acts of assault on women by their peers, and young women continue to refrain from reporting assaults. *Family Guy* is a good example of rape jokes. In one episode, the character Peter is watching a news program where the anchor is reporting the rape of three college students. He quips: "Aw, man. See that? Everybody's gettin' laid but me." (Media Education Foundation 2011: 17).

One further effect of masculinity policing and the bro code is that if a Bro is witness to an assault incident, he knows he must keep his mouth closed (Media Education Foundation 2011) – "bros before hoes" means that women are fair game, and all bros stick together. Keith (cited in Media Education Foundation 2011: 20) argues that "much of male culture is taught that women are disposable, that women 'ask for it', and that getting a woman drunk so that you can take advantage of her is just part of having a good time".

A survey of posts to EverydaySexism.com suggests that women have not learned to recognize assault in many cases, and even when they do, they do not feel entitled to report it. In many cases where they do report it, their experience is diminished or belittled. The survey, which I conducted between August 12–16, 2013, covered the most recent 1000 posts to the site, the earliest of which was dated June 26, 2013. Posts are anonymous, although some posters used a female first name, and as most of them are drawn from an associated Twitter account, the majority were "tweet length" (140 characters or less). The resulting analysis found 31 different categories of sexist behaviour, including eight different kinds of sexual assault, and 11 different kinds of verbal abuse. The posts were made by women from across the globe, though there was no way other than use of particular words (such as "tube" to refer to a train) to identify from which countries the posts originated. Many of the posts appeared to originate from the UK and USA, but there were also posters from other parts of Europe, Australia and New Zealand. A significant number of posts were badly written, with poor grammar and syntax, but it is impossible to know whether this is because the posters' first language was other than English or whether there was some other factor involved, such as poor education, use of "text speak" or simply bad typing. Some of the posters, though by far the minority, identified their age. The youngest identified herself as 11, while the oldest reported that she was in her fifties. All but two of the posts appeared to be from unique posters, though again, there is no way of being certain.

The types of sexual assault reported were: being groped in public places such as the tube/train or in a club, having a man masturbate in front of you (for example in an otherwise empty tube carriage), touching of clothes and hair by a strange man, standing close and ejaculating against a woman's leg on the tube, a strange man putting his hand down a woman's pants, again on the train, flashing genitals at women and girls in various venues and date rape. Verbal insults included wolf whistles, sexual invitations from strangers in the street such as "Do you suck cock?" "Get your tits out," and "Show me where you pee", insults from men in cars after being ignored, such as "boner killer" or "I would never fuck you", being referred to at work as "sexretary" or "eye candy", being called a lesbian as a derogatory term, young boys who are virgins being told to "fuck a drunk slut" to prove they're not gay, men shouting rape threats in the street when ignored, referring to women and girls as "bitches", being called a "feminazi", men turning nasty when their advances are rejected with insults such as "You're an ugly cunt, who'd want to fuck you anyway?", "tease" and "slut", and asking "how much?" of a woman who is waiting in the street.

There was significant evidence of denial in cases of date rape and sexual harassment, with women being told "not to make waves" and "boys will be boys" when complaining of sexual harassment, being told that date rape was just "a bad hookup", repeatedly being told to "suck it up" even when traumatized, because "it's your word against his" or "no one will believe you". One woman reported seeing comments such as "get back in the kitchen" on a Facebook science site in response to an image of a female scientist. Another woman reported that leggings were banned in her high school because they were considered "sexual harassment" of the male teachers, and yet another woman reported that men assumed she was "easy" because she was Asian. There was also a recurrent theme of women repeatedly being told to be quiet. Another significant theme was people standing by and watching while sexual harassment or assault occurred. One woman reported being harassed by primary school boys. Finally, there were many, many reports of women feeling unsafe and scared.

Clearly, sexism, sexual harassment and sexual assault are everyday occurrences in our society, and yet denial of all three dominates the public narrative. The above themes suggest that women are regarded as public property, there to be used for men's sexual enjoyment at their leisure. Girls as young as 11 are being catcalled and harassed on the streets and in schools, and there is a sense of entitlement among some men at least that they can touch and feel women, that they can gaze at them and parts of their bodies indiscriminately and without pretence, that they can loudly discuss them and their body parts as if they were inanimate objects incapable of hearing. Blaming the victim is also a common theme, for example, for looking "hot", for being out after dark or for wearing certain clothes. Women are thus made the gatekeepers for men's sexuality, requiring them to dress down, stay indoors, block their ears and become invisible, if they do not want to be subjected to unwanted sexual advances by men. Underlying all this is the assumption that a woman's role is to be subservient to men both at work and in public and be available for sex whenever and wherever a man pleases.

Conclusion

Men tend to take up space, they emit and produce. They move around freely and take what they want and need as an entitlement. Women, on the other hand, are not entitled to occupy public space except under certain conditions. Those conditions comprise a series of binaries: for example, being available for men's use or else being invisible. When a woman occupies public space in a way that men notice, they must assume that she is available and ready for sex. Women who rebel against this code are labelled "feminazis" and either silenced or shown exactly what it is they "really" want. The geography of sexual space, then, is dominated by male presence, while women and girls float in and out depending on whether and how much they are ready to abide by the code. Otherwise, they must stay indoors or find a way to proceed unnoticed. Sexual space is also dominated by the male gaze, while women's eyes must remain downcast or looking away into the distance. A woman's direct gaze is interpreted as an invitation for sex, so if she wants otherwise, she must avert her gaze, pretend to be vacant, for it is only as vacant, invisible and deaf that she is safe. All this speaks to men's "need for sex and women's compliance from a position of passivity" (O'Brien et al. 2013: 130), "men's demand for sex as a biological imperative" (O'Brien et al. 2013: 133), and of "normalizing the male demand [while] removing the woman's agency" (O'Brien et al. 2013: 136).

7
Sexual Predation and Gendered Norms

Introduction

This chapter explores the concept of the sexual predator and how it relates to gendered subjectivities and love distortion. Contemporary discourses suggest that women cannot be predators and men cannot be victims. Females are almost always victims in the public eye; males can only be victims if they are children – and the line between childhood and manhood is very fine indeed. Transition between childhood and manhood is often crossed fairly abruptly. Males tend to go from being little asexual boys to pubescent young men in a very short space of time, their deepening voice, facial and body hair, and increased bulk a clear delineation of manhood and an indication of readiness for sexual activity (Driscoll 2002; Care Notes 2013). Females on the other hand, tend to transition to womanhood much more slowly, equivocating back and forth over a number of years.

> A girl never becomes a woman in any univocal or unidirectional sense. Feminine adolescence is not a transition from one state to another but a contingent and in some senses reversible movement.
>
> (Driscoll 2002: 198)

Thus a boy's transition to puberty is much more obvious than that of a girl's, and this may be part of the issue surrounding women's and girls' victimhood. Very young women and girls may appear to be and act much older than their age, while grown women often appear much younger, dress younger or adopt girlish mannerisms. I will argue that much bad behaviour by women is attributed to vulnerability and emotional immaturity, that women offenders, especially sex offenders, tend to be infantilized by the criminal justice system, the media and the general public.

The aim of this chapter is to challenge contemporary discourses about gender and sexual predation by exploring the ways in which we construct sex offenders, specifically, female sex offenders. While male sex offenders are always cast as predators, female sex offenders are often made out to be victims, given the vulnerable role (Hayes and Carpenter 2013). While this appears to be in direct conflict with the arguments of the previous chapter, where I discussed the pervasiveness and insidiousness of sexism in our society, I will argue that it is actually in keeping with the sexist view of women because it infantilizes them and constrains their subjectivity.

Who is the sex offender?

Since the media "discovery" of the paedophile in the 1990s, sex abuse against children has dominated the press (Thomas 2005) and the popular imagination. What is most important, however, is the overwhelmingly popular belief that the sex offender is exclusively male. Indeed, given that the majority of research fails to even contemplate the female sex offender (Landor 2009), it is reasonable to conclude that in the public psyche as well as in the knowledge domains of academia, the sex offender is male. However, there is an emerging body of international and Australian research that challenges this perception, particularly with respect to child sexual abuse.

Research to date indicates that it is difficult to determine prevalence of sexual abuse due to high levels of under-reporting (Hayes and Carpenter 2013; Denov 2003; Braveheart 2009; Neame and Heenan 2003), and this necessarily impacts on what we know about the gender of sex offenders. Nevertheless, "official statistics" do exist and generally indicate that the majority of sex offenders are male and most victims female (Gavin 2005). As a result, most sex offending research has focused on male perpetrators and female victims (Landor 2009; Thomas 2005; Denov 2003; Vandiver and Walker 2003). Recent statistics, however, show an increase in numbers of both convicted female sex offenders and male victims under 16. Boroughs (2004), for example, reports that in the USA in the late 1990s official statistics show that women made up 25 per cent of convicted abusers of children under 16. In the UK, The Lucy Faithful Foundation reported in 2009 that up to 30 per cent of sexual abusers of children under 16 are women (cited in Townsend and Syal 2009). Gleb (2007: 16) reports that of the 853 sex offenders adjudicated in Magistrates Courts across Australia in 2004–2005, only 12 were women, although these statistics were not broken down according to age of victim, and there are no statistics to date reporting the numbers of female paedophiles in Australia. Again in the Australian arena, MAKO, a website devoted to identifying sex offenders in Australia, reports that out of "over 1500" identified offenders, only 29 are female. However, the methodology for arriving at these figures is unclear. Nathan and Ward (2002) report that the official rate for Australia is 5 per cent of all sexual offences against children, but that the true number is thought to be considerably higher. The fact that Australian statistics tend to be far lower than those reported in the USA and UK suggests there are some anomalies in the way that official statistics are kept in this country, or that female sexual abuse is highly under-reported, or both.

Factors impacting on the under-reporting of sexual offences include embarrassment, self-blame, fear of further victimization by legal processes, lack of confidence in the criminal justice system, disruption to the family unit, perceptions of low impact of damage and the fact that for some young people (especially males), sexual precocity is seen as a rite of passage (Denov 2003; Deering and Mellor 2011). What little research there is on female sex offenders suggests that victims of sexual abuse – especially child victims – may be more reluctant to report being accosted by a female than by a male (Davidson 2008). Nevertheless, while the official picture of the ratio of male to female sex offenders suggests that women offend less, there is considerable speculation in the media and among those working in the field that numbers of female offenders are increasing (e.g. Townsend and Syal 2009). To date, there has been little other research comparing sex offenders or victims based on gender, age or sexuality, or exploring discrepancies in sentencing. Additionally, in spite of the flawed nature of official statistics, these same statistics inform current policy and practice, which therefore remains ignorant of, and blind to the impact of, female sexual offences against children.

In a world in which children are regarded as highly vulnerable and at risk, child sex offenders are regarded as dangerous and predatory. However, given the above observations, it is not surprising that male offenders are regarded as more dangerous than females. This chapter explores the ways in which people think about female sex offenders and whether they perceive them as being culpable in the same way as male offenders. This is important because, if child sexual abuse perpetrated by women is not perceived as a crime, then such abuse will be vastly under-reported. Where there is the perception of crime, if it is not seen as serious (in the same way that child sexual crimes perpetrated by men are seen as serious), then there is no impetus to develop relevant and appropriate treatment programs for female sex offenders. Indeed, Hayes et al. (2012) note that in at least one instance, a judge refused to impose a custodial sentence on a female sex offender precisely because there were no such treatment or rehabilitation programs available in prisons in Australia. Finally, if culpability of female offenders is regarded as low among jurors, then fairness in sentencing is called into question.

These observations are significant because it suggests a need for an analysis of female sex offending outside the dominant discourses, which essentialize women as naturally caring, nurturing and non-criminal. Many female sex offenders do not seem to be regarded as dangerous predators or as risky in the same sense that male offenders are (Hayes et al. 2011) and receive less public disapproval than male sex offenders in the same situation (Hayes et al. 2012). This gendered social response is the impetus for the research reported in this chapter, which it is hoped offers new insights into the female sex offender, who, while in the minority of all sex offenders, remains an under-scrutinized subject of research.

Invisibility of the female offender

The "discovery" of female sexual offending in the 1990s in a small number of psychological studies in the USA, Canada and the UK, struggled with issues of prevalence, positioning it as a rare phenomenon. Many of these studies concluded that female sexual offending is "an aberration which has little or no significance for professionals working with child sexual abuse" (Denov 2004: 303). The Diagnostic and Statistical Manual of Mental Disorders 4th Edition concludes that acts of paraphilia (which include paedophilia) "are almost never diagnosed in females" (Denov 2004: 303). According to Landor (2009), given that the vast majority of research on sex offenders fails to even contemplate the female sex offender, it is reasonable to conclude that in the public psyche as well as in the knowledge domains of the academic community, the predatory sex offender is a male, regardless of how many cases of female sex offending are brought before the courts or reported in the media.

Although there are pockets of research emerging internationally that are challenging the research focus purely on the male sexual offender, there is still much to be done in this area. Common themes emerging from this body of work include acknowledging that the prevalence of female sex offending is much higher than current statistics suggest, recognition of high levels of underreporting of child sexual abuse in general, which impacts on female prevalence, and differential understandings of the severity and impact of female sex offending. Across the board, researchers and professionals working in the field of child sexual abuse acknowledge the invisibility of the female sex offender, and the ramifications of such invisibility for research, programs, policy and practice. However, apart from the psychological literature, this group remains largely uncritiqued, due to the perceived low offending rates and/or women's diversion from the criminal justice system (Denov 2004; Gakhal and Brown 2011; Cortoni and Gannon 2011).

Reoffending and harm

While the limited research available indicates that there is very little difference in risk of reoffending between male and female sex offenders, it is surprising that female offenders are regarded as less dangerous. For example, Freeman and Sandler's (2008) research on 780 male and female sex offenders in New York City indicated that although male sex offenders were more likely to be rearrested than female sex offenders, there were limited differences in terms of actual risk factors. If we assume that risk of reoffending positively correlates with perceptions of dangerousness, then this perception of female sex offenders as less risky or dangerous is spurious. Hayes et al. (2013) found that, where women are convicted of child sexual offences in both Australia and the UK, they tend to fall into two categories. Women who abuse young children under the age of 12 are vilified in much the same way as dangerous male offenders, but do not appear to be regarded as dangerous in the same ways as a male perpetrator of similar crimes. Women who abuse pubescent and adolescent children often receive much lighter sentences than their male counterparts, and may or may not be required to sign a sex offender register. For example, a female teacher in Victoria, convicted of abuse of a 15-year-old male student, received a 22-month suspended sentence, while a male teacher who abused a 14-year-old female student was sentenced to two years and two months in prison. This raises several questions: do the courts (and the public) perceive that (1) less harm was done by the female offender, or (2) that she poses less risk of reoffending, or (3) that young male victims are harmed less by sexual abuse than their female counterparts or (4) that some combination of all these perceptions underlies such determinations?

The lack of consistent evidence-based research

These questions from the literature and from practice denote the need for further consistent evidence-based research. For example, inconsistency of methods and sample sizes in undertaking research on female sexual offending and its impact on victims has resulted in contradictory data and research outcomes (Saradjian and Hanks 2010; Cortoni and Gannon 2011; Deering and Mellor 2011). Further research investigating attitudes towards sex offenders has failed to specify the gender of the sex offenders (Gakhal and Brown 2011). In particular, there is inconsistency in findings of prevalence of female sex offending, and most of what is available comes out of the USA. Cortoni et al. (2009), for example, estimated that 1 in 20 child sex offenders are female, while Fauske et al. (2006) cite studies that indicate women perpetrators accounted for nearly 43 per cent of all educator sexual misconduct in the US schooling system.

Public perceptions of sex offenders

Current research on public perceptions of sex offenders is scant, and most of what exists is decades old (Fuselier et al. 2002: 272). For example, Wurtele et al. (1992) found that while 90 per cent of parents warned their children about strangers, only a few parents described child sex offenders as known adults, adolescents or siblings. In a study of US jurors, Morrison and Greene (1992) report that 20 per cent believe the stereotype of an abuser as a "dirty old man". They state that "identifying public perceptions of perpetrators is significant for developing public education about CSA [child sexual abuse]" (Wurtele et al. 1992: 272) and yet there has been very little recent work in the area, and none at all relating to female sex offenders.

Current discourses conceptualize sex offending around discussions of harm, subjectivity and gender. In general, there appear to be two main discourses – the feminist and the psychological – that theorize these phenomena. In particular, the rise of feminism mid-last century was crucial to the identification of child sexual abuse. In its early, essentialist form, it was premised on male domination and female victimization, and positioned predatory males along a sexual continuum where all males have the potential and perhaps even propensity under the right circumstances to become sexual predators (Gleb 2007). It challenged psychological accounts that position male sexual predators as aberrations, while at the same time positioning women as essentially victims of male patriarchal control (Scully 1994; Chung et al. 2006; Hayes et al. 2012). Of course, there has been much feminist work done since that largely departs from this crude model to take account of the more nuanced relationships and subjectivities generated by constructions of gender and sexuality (e.g. Carrington and Perreira 2009; Renzetti 2009). However, it remains that much public policy and legislation concerning violence in general and sexual violence in particular, still draws its rationale from the cruder picture of the patriarchal social stratus. One only need look at the recent Australian campaign against domestic violence, the slogan for which was "To violence against women, Australia says no", (Ball and Hayes 2011), not to mention the even more telling predominance of offender treatment and prevention programs directed entirely at men.

The psychological discourse, on the other hand, while also essentializing sexual offending, links that offending closely to sexuality (Angelides 2007). Child sexual abuse is typically not a one-off, an aberration or mistake. Paedophiles are considered to be, by their essential nature, at high risk of reoffending. In this sense, the attraction to children under the age of consent is just a characteristic of their sexuality, in much the same way that same-sex attraction is a sexuality – only the paedophile is more sinister because his attraction is one that involves the exercise of masculine power and control over subjects who are unable to consent. It is for this reason that "true" female paedophiles are seen as rare. Women's subjective experience as victims requires that even when they offend they do so under pressure and in ways that are out of their control because they are damaged or somehow traumatized (Hayes and Carpenter 2013).

Thus, the female sex offender is virtually absent from most mainstream theoretical discourse. Where it has been acknowledged as a potential problem, as noted above, such reports come from a fairly straightforward understanding of subjectivity via traditional sexual scripts. Angelides (2007: 360), for example, in his research on subjectivity in a case study concerning the adolescent male victim of a female offender, reports that the offender was excused for having "marriage difficulties". Indeed, he states that "the judge concluded that she was 'vulnerable to...flirtation and succumbed to it'", positioning the adolescent "victim" as the predator. Indeed, the victim himself claims to have "initiated the relationship", claiming the masculine subjectivity attributable to the predator, and virtually dismissing, if not vigorously denying any victimhood at all (Angelides 2007: 360).

Where women are convicted as offenders, they are often excused or their behaviours explained in ways that deny them any subjectivity at all. In the UK, for example, Vanessa George, who in 2009 was convicted of abusing toddlers in her care, was described as damaged and traumatized, the victim of a troubled childhood, and her offences as merely an accomplice to a man (Hayes and Carpenter 2013). In this way, women who offend with others often are explained through the simple existence of a male companion or dominant male by whom she is coerced or upon whom she is emotionally dependent. George's offences were committed as part of an internet paedophile ring which included two other women, and yet, neither of the other women were vilified and analysed in the press and by the public in the same way as George. This could be attributed to the fact that George is not traditionally attractive, is overweight and a carer of children in a nursery, a job that carries with it certain expectations of nurturing and safety. George's predatory behaviour towards children in her care is all the more horrifying because it lays bare the shocking possibility of a mother figure acting thus.

When offending alone, women's behaviour is understood through the lens of vulnerability and trauma, discourses that are never made available to male offenders in the same positions. For example, Karen Louise Ellis, who was found guilty in an Australian court of sexual offences against a 15-year-old boy, was described by the judge as "emotionally immature" and the victim of a strained marriage (Angelides 2007). For women, public discourses work to return her to a normative frame of femininity – rarely are men seen so sympathetically (Hayes and Carpenter 2013).

This chapter draws on my earlier theoretical work to explain the nexus between sex, gender and taboo surrounding sexual predation (Hayes et al. 2012). Moral judgements about sex and what is considered taboo change over time, as do the kinds of justifications that are employed in support of changing moralities. Morality also shapes law over time, fabricating fairly tenuous justifications from within socially constructed communities of practice that are subject to ongoing change (Hayes et al. 2012). Thus, what is considered taboo reflects the conventional morality of the historic period. At various times and places in history, for example, sexual relationships between young women/girls and much older men were considered acceptable, even the norm. In the 1800s, the age of consent for young women in England was 12, enacted in the 1861 *Offences Against the Person Act* (Smart 1992: 26). Young men were explicitly excluded from the Act, presumably because consent wasn't seen to be an issue for them. Of course, later that century, the age of consent was raised to 16, as it was in Australia a short time later – although in Australia, girls of 14 and 15 were excluded if they "looked sixteen" (Allen 1990: 79). The development of a specific cut-off line where childhood and vulnerability ends and adulthood begins has therefore waxed and waned somewhat over time.

As mentioned in Chapter 3 above, historians such as Aries (1973) argue that childhood in Westernized industrialized countries only came to be regarded as a distinct developmental phase in the sixteenth century. It wasn't until industrialization took a firm hold, making child labour an anachronism, that children began to be seen as objects of affection and care. At the same time, children came to be seen as completely different to adults, as innocent and essentially uncorrupted. By the latter decades of the twentieth century, children had achieved a status of vulnerability unrivalled in any other era. Childhood has now extended into the teenage years via the concept of adolescence (Aries 1973).

An imaginary (and largely ad hoc) age-line has been drawn which demarcates children from adults. Within this conceptualization, anyone who is labelled a child must not be exposed to the sexual mores of those who are on the other side of that line. This age-line not only fluctuates legally between jurisdictions, but also tends to fluctuate according to gender. The difference in cultural values and beliefs about sex gives us some indication of the relative arbitrariness of the age-lines drawn between childhood and adulthood. This historical and contextual overview helps us to understand our current moral panic about sex and children, but it does not really explain why we understand the older "child" victim of sexual abuse differently, depending on the gender of the predator.

Gendered sexual performances are embedded in cultural norms about sexuality and reflect gender stereotypes and behavioural expectations (see Chapter 5 above). Men are perceived as naturally more aggressive and have the active role in sexual relationships. It is difficult to perceive men as sexually reluctant or as victims of sexual coercion or assault (Denov 2003). The traditional feminine script is one that emphasizes idealism, passivity and virtue. The female in this script is sexually passive and innocent, sexually harmless and neither sexually aggressive nor an initiator of sex (Weiderman 2005). Sexual scripts also apply to children, as we saw above in Chapter 3. Healthy children are asexual. Children with sexual knowledge are victims. There is no place for a discussion of the body functionality of children in sexual terms (Kaye 2005). These scripts complicate further as generational lines are crossed. The way adults who engage in sex with children are represented depends on their gender and the gender of the child.

The tension between desire and taboo creates an undercurrent of distrust surrounding young girls while at the same time blurring the line for boys. The mistrust surrounding girls speaks to their sexual potential as well as to the perceived inability of adults – particularly male adults – to regard young bodies as anything but sexual. Conversely, young men are taught that the primary manifestation and demonstration of masculinity is an overt attraction to girls and women, with little differentiation being made between the two.

This chapter further explores this phenomenon by analysing public discourses reported in the media. The following sections describe respectively the methodology employed in this process and the findings and analysis of that research.

Media analysis

For the purposes of this research, a study of public perceptions of female sex offending was conducted through an analysis of media reports collected from mainstream news media in both Australia and the UK. These two locations were chosen for the similarities in culture, convention and social mores, but also based on the relative differences in levels of recognition of female sex offending between the two nations. Female sex offenders are more apparent in media and other public discourses in the UK compared to Australia, suggesting that Australians are yet to "catch up" to the UK in recognizing female sex offenders as an issue. Disparities in statistics described above in the background literature also suggest that victims of female sex offenders may be more reluctant to report in Australia due to that lack of recognition. The current media analysis is not intended to test either of those preliminary hypotheses – indeed, a much larger and more directed survey of public opinion is required for such research. Rather, the following analysis seeks to explore public discourses surrounding female sex offenders to identify possible themes, as well as any similarities and/or differences between the two locations.

News articles were collected from online print media, including *The Guardian, The Times, The Observer, The Daily Mail,* syndicated press reports (for example from Associated Newspapers, The Press Association and News Ltd) and independent press reports in smaller news media sites in the UK. In Australia, reports were collected from *The Age, The Sydney Morning Herald, The Australian, The Courier Mail, Northern Territory News* and syndicated press reports from AAP Australian Associated News Wire reported on smaller news sites and accessed through the Australia/New Zealand Reference Centre database. The timeframe for the data collection was 2000 through 2010 (n = 485).

Of the 485 news articles collected, 76 were discarded as being unrelated to the current research, specifically where a woman was mentioned in relation to a sex offence but was not charged or arrested for any offence. In addition, 17 articles were general reports about female sex offenders including reports of research being published on the issue or comments by public figures of a general nature. Of the remaining reports, 290 were reports of pre-pubescent abuse and 102 were reports of abuse against pubescent and adolescent children.

My initial coding divided the reports into two groups – those concerned with pre-pubescent victims (aged 11 years and under) and those concerning pubescent and adolescent offenders (aged 12–16). Coding was done manually by reading through the reports and identifying common and/or popularly used terms, phrases and themes used in describing female sex offenders, their crimes and their victims. The coding did not count these terms, phrases or themes, but was more concerned with identifying common themes and the general tone of both the comments made about female sex offenders and their crimes and the reporting of those comments and crimes. The articles were then more deeply interrogated as discourses to identify overt and covert patterns of reference to harm, subjectivity and gender, which were key theoretical concepts informing the research. This critical analysis is informed by what Graham (2005) describes as the "discursive analytic". While not a method in and of itself – unlike what Taylor (2004) refers to as Critical Discourse Analysis – this discursive analytic informs my methodology by lighting the way for a "journey and conversation" with the media reporters of female sex offenders as well as the participants in the conversations and observations reported (Graham 2005: 2). This discursive analytic is therefore not necessarily generalizable; rather it provides the impetus for identifying contradictions and anomalies that may be useful in developing some more grounded research questions for further empirical research.

Gendered narratives

In the pre-pubescent group, findings revealed a total of 41 individual female sex offenders had been identified across Australia and the UK. Two of those were named Australian offenders and 24 were named offenders in the UK. A total of 3 Australian women and 11 UK women were unnamed. In the pubescent/adolescent group, there were a total of 74 individual female sex offenders, including 6 named Australian and 40 named British. Within this second group, 11 British women and 14 Australian women were unnamed.

Out of these totals, several of the offenders dominated. In the UK, Vanessa George and her accomplices were most prominent, while in Australia it was Karen Louise Ellis. As we have already noted, both offenders have been identified in numerous scholarly articles. The contrast between these two cases is instructive, so I will explore these in some detail.

In 2009, Vanessa George was convicted of abusing toddlers in her care while working in a nursery in the UK. Media reports described George as an accomplice to a male ringleader of a technology-based paedophile ring, even though she clearly acted out her offences alone and often. During her trial, she was vilified and demonized by both the public and the media. Described as "unnatural", "a monster" and "sickening", George was commonly regarded as an affront to mother-hood and all that women represent. One parent commented, "I want to rip off her skin and roll her in salt!" But, as mentioned earlier in this chapter, she was also excused for her behaviour in many ways. Reports of a traumatized childhood, the loss of her mother early on and later involvement in the paranormal set George up as a tragic figure destined for a tragic end. In the eyes of the media and the public she was also a victim, and her victimhood is what caused her to act against her "feminine nature". If the feminine is understood, as we saw above, as sexually passive and innocent, sexually harmless and neither sexually aggressive nor an initiator of sex (Weiderman 2005), then there must be some essential flaw in George, a blip on an otherwise normal feminine façade.

Many of the reports about George mention her taking photographs of the toddlers in her care while she was changing their nappies – presumably the photographs were of their genitals, though none of the reports confirm this. Here we see a blurring of the line between motherly caretaking and sick voyeurism, another issue that is reported to be coming to the attention of police, the courts and the public in recent years. Parents may find some innocent parental joy in taking pictures of their children naked – indeed there is a long tradition in art that celebrates the naked child – but the naked child is not meant to be fodder for desire, and cases such as George's raise questions about where to draw the line between innocence and taboo. The fact that George was circulating these pictures among her accomplices clearly indicates some sinister intention, and there lies the difference. Where a parent's intention is purely sentimental, the taboo loses strength. Yet, we are becoming nervous about anyone taking pictures of naked children. I would argue that this aversion to the image of a naked child stems from a fear of the adult gaze, which can only look upon a naked body with desire. Concomitantly, what the adult desires, it is in danger of acting upon; thus, even an intention that is innocent cannot escape the taboo, for it is always in danger of turning "bad" (Hayes et al. 2012).

When we contrast George's case with that of Australian teacher, Karen Louise Ellis, however, we observe several surprising differences. In 2008, Ellis was charged with six counts of sexual penetration of a 15-year-old male student, with whom she had had an affair. Nevertheless, the court chose to see her not as a predator, or even an aberration; rather, she was depicted as vulnerable and emotionally immature, but largely harmless (Angelides 2007). Moreover, her "victim" refused to be identified as such, claiming that he initiated the affair and that it had no ill effects on him. He stated, "I have been in a sexual relationship before Karen. At no stage has this affected my life." (Angelides 2007). Although the boy was consistently denied any subjecthood throughout the case, the judge concluded that he was not substantially harmed. Ellis, on the other hand, was painted as an attractive, relatively young woman with a troubled marriage who was taken advantage of. The fact that she had actual intercourse with the boy seemed to carry no weight whatsoever in the initial court proceedings. Compared to George, who was vilified for taking photographs of her victims, Ellis appears almost saintly – albeit misguided. This enormous discrepancy between constructions of offence, offender and victims in these cases suggests that there are markers of both age and gender that demarcate taboo in cases of child sexual abuse.

Intergenerational sex, harm and female subjectivity

My analysis of the media reports revealed that, in the case of pre-pubescent victims, most women offenders acted with or were associated with a male offender, and were cast as his "accomplice". The majority of articles on George depict her as an accomplice to Colin Blanchard, along with Allen and Dawber, two other women involved in the "ring". Intimations of vulnerability and manipulation by the male "ringleader" suggest that these women's behaviour may be excused on some level, or at the very least made coherent.

Almost in the same sentence, however, they are painted as "horrific", "evil", their deeds the "ultimate female betrayal", and the discourses offered by the public when asked for comment were of the nature of "a mother wouldn't do that". In this latter sense, these women were vilified even more than their male counterparts – tried twice, as women offenders often are, in a "trial by gender" – once by the courts, and then again by the media and the public.

One interesting aspect of these discourses was the attention paid to the physical appearance of some of the female offenders – especially when they were relatively young and attractive. For example, Allen's appearance and dress were described in reports of the court proceedings thus: "Allen, who was wearing a gold scarf, spoke only to confirm her name..." Photos of George, on the other hand, show her as a dumpy, unstylish woman, and her appearance is never described. Attractiveness in relation to female offenders therefore offers another perplexing discourse – here is a woman who is considered "evil" and "unnatural" and yet we have stopped to consider her state of dress. This attention to appearance suggests that the public should be doubly shocked by a woman who abuses children if she is also attractive, perhaps intimating that an attractive women would have other recourse to satisfy her desires. Similarly, the marital and motherly status of female offenders of both pre-pubescent and post-pubescent/adolescent victims is often described. Indeed, headlines will often report along the lines of "Mother of two abuses toddler in her care...", again intimating the shock of abuse that is performed by someone who should be informed by an ethic of nurturing, caring and child safety.

In the case of female sexual offenders of pubescent/adolescent victims (where the victim is a boy), however – and these are often teachers, coaches, friends' mothers and so on – the discourse of vulnerability and trauma trumps discourses of predation and intention by the offender. These offenders are infantilized, depicted as "emotionally immature", "psychologically impaired", their "marriage on the rocks". They are often seen as victims of problematic marriages and other trauma. In contrast, their young male victims are often regarded as "lucky" (to be able to access sexual experience from an older woman), especially when he's 14–16 years old and claims to have suffered little or no harm.

However, where the victim of a female offender is a teenage girl, the girl retains the victim status, and the offender becomes a predator, although never to the extent of a male offender under similar circumstances. Again, reports of such offences often describe the offender's appearance. In the UK, for example, reports of a young female tennis coach who seduced her 13-year-old charge, describe her as young, blonde and athletic. These findings reflect an inherent and universal meaning of particular sex offences on the one hand, and a genderized view of sex offences on the other. Child sexual abuse is universally considered to be abhorrent and yet the ambivalence surrounding teenage victims suggests some uncertainty about the status of the victim-as-child, including the victim's self-perception in each case. Female adolescent sexuality prioritizes fear and risk, and silences desire and pleasure for female victims, while the female offender who embodies successful femininity and youth is infantilized, made vulnerable and passive, thus excusing her transgressive behaviour. Male adolescent sexuality, on the other hand, draws on dominant masculine scripts valorizing sex with experienced older women, even while those same masculine scripts are reviled where they are employed by the male predator of young women. Clearly there is no little confusion about the meaning of masculine and feminine, and how individuals may draw on traditional scripts when determining their victimhood or their masculinized power.

Role of the media

Throughout the study it is clear that the media is a crucial campaigner for the victim, even while also being a source of the sexualization of children. Media reports have the capacity to also create news from the bare bones of a situation or alleged crime, often drawing inferences where they are not necessarily warranted, or using innuendo to suggest intent or to pinhole a victim's or offender's subjectivity. The media also create news by releasing the identities of sex offenders and paedophiles, which works to incite hysteria surrounding child sexual abuse and the existence of sexual predators in the community.

The issue of mandatory harm in child sexual abuse is also juxtaposed against the mitigating vulnerabilities of female offenders, in some cases letting them off the hook, or at the very least excusing or explaining their offences. Though this research did not analyse

reports of male sex offenders, as we have seen, the scholarly literature suggests that male offenders do not receive the same privilege.
My analysis, however, found that females who abuse young children
are painted as monstrous, often more so than men, because they have
denied their role as natural protectors of children. Thus the media
plays an important role in exacerbating the contradictions inherent in current gendered discourses surrounding child sexual abuse,
childhood and adolescence, as well as masculinity and femininity.
On the one hand, children are depicted as sexually innocent, subject to long-term harm when exposed to sexual activity too early in
their development. Sexual activity provides the implicit demarcation
between childhood and adulthood (Aries 1973), and discourses are
fraught with fear surrounding the perceived early crossing of that
boundary. The contradiction is even more pronounced in discourses
depicting differing subjectivities of the victims and offenders depending on age and gender. Here, victim subjectivities range from harmed
victim to sexual initiator, while offender subjectivities range from
sexual predator to sexually passive. These subjectivities rely both on
bodily performance and functionality – the active versus the passive,
sexual predator versus sexually reluctant, sexual exploration versus
sexual gatekeeper.

In many cases femininity is defined *against* the sexual, even where
victimhood is denied, though admittedly that is rare. The female
almost always must be the victim, regardless of how she identifies.
The subjective experience of the male adolescent, however, is based
almost entirely on sexual performance and masculine prowess and
cannot in many cases, therefore, access the victim script.

Conclusion

Although there are pockets of research emerging internationally that
are challenging the research focus purely on the male sexual offender,
there is still much to be done in this area. Common themes emerging
from this body of work include acknowledging that the prevalence of
female sex offending is much higher than current statistics suggest,
recognition of high levels of under-reporting of child sexual abuse in
general, which impacts on female prevalence, and differential understandings of the severity and impact of female sex offending. Across
the board, researchers and professionals working in the field of child

sexual abuse acknowledge the invisibility of the female sex offender, and the ramifications of such invisibility for research, programs, policy and practice. Apart from the psychological literature, this group remains largely uncritiqued, due to the perceived low offending rates and/or women's diversion from the criminal justice system (Denov 2004; Cortoni and Gannon 2011; Gakhal and Brown 2011). Hopefully, the gaps in research addressed by my analysis will provide a useful contribution to knowledge about female sex offenders and their impact on society as a whole, as well as an impetus to further thinking about gender, sexuality and crime, particularly the ways in which both men and women are governed by heteronormative gender roles and sexual scripts, and their attempts at resistance, I suggest, rendered powerless.

8
Conclusion – A Geography of Abuse

Introduction

This chapter aims to provide a summary of sorts of the arguments made in the preceding chapters, and attempts to draw the threads of those arguments together in order to make sense of the nexus of sex, love and abuse. In Chapter 6, I discussed an article in *Maxim* magazine titled "How to Cure a Feminist". Interestingly, a poem by the same title by performance poet, Kait Rokowski, provides an interesting counterpoint. Rokowski cleverly (and sarcastically) outlines the eight steps a man should go through to cure his woman of any empowerment. Step 1 requires replacing the word "tits" with the word "equality" ("I love equality!"); Step 2 asks him to make her jealous; Step 3, to insult her in a way that makes her think you are complimenting her; Step 4 says, "keep her on a diet of cigarettes and hairspray until her waist is an apple core", and so on. Each step becomes more sarcastic and telling of the sexist brainwashing women are often subjected to, culminating in Step 8:

> *Step 8: Give her a new name.*
> *First, whisper it in the crook of her neck til her*
>   *muscles have committed it to memory*
> *Then shout it in the belly of her bedroom*
>   *til the echo haunts her sleep*
> *Finally, scratch it into her back when you fuck her,*
>   *like branding your favourite ball gag*
> *It is proof that nothing is sacred, that no backbone*
>   *is too straight to be snapped into submission*

Every layer of skin can be clawed off
Nothing before this mattered
She never even existed without you.[1]

I have no idea whether Rokowski's poem is a direct response to *Maxim*, or whether it occurred coincidently at around the same time. What I do know is that both events are symptomatic of a wider gender struggle currently playing out in our Western world, in which the backlash against feminism is gaining ground. How much more ground it will claim depends upon the level of social and political complacency that is allowed to endure. In Chapter 1, I discussed how philosophy is not antithetical to the political – rather, it can and should be a stepping-stone towards it. As well as being a philosophical and sociological analysis of some aspects of that gender struggle, then, the foregoing chapters are a call to action. That call is a long time coming, but it joins the voices that can already be heard in the near distance via feminist performers such as Kait Rokowski and Lily Myers, feminist scholars such as Claire Renzetti and Kerry Carrington, initiatives such as the Everyday Sexism Project and the groundswell of women and men throughout the West who are speaking out against sexism, misogyny and violence.

This book has focused on abuse of women. Although it traces the impact of sexism, misogyny and discourses of love distortion on women and girls, these issues impact intersectionally. Sexism, racism, classism, homophobia, transphobia and misogyny are all inherent characteristics of our Western society, all equally as urgent in their need to be addressed, and – as a result – abuse is endemic. The world is changing at an exponential rate. As I was growing up in the 1960s and 70s I witnessed the civil rights and women's liberation movements at first hand. While women were burning their bras and letting their hair down, people of colour were beginning to be allowed to share in the greater prosperity that had previously been owned completely by privileged white people. It was an inspiring time, and also a frightening one, with recreational drug use skyrocketing and the contraceptive pill making "free love" available to women as well as men. It took some time for society to realize that we needed to figure out exactly what we were to do with all this. Sadly, we still do not know.

This book has attempted to highlight some of the more elusive issues concerning gender, sexuality, violence and abuse, namely, why women accept being abused or fail to leave, how destructive discourses of romance are to our relationships and personal subjectivities, how our desires are often in tension with our need for empowerment, and how ubiquitous sexism and misogyny is in a society in which everyone is supposed to be equal – issues that one reviewer of this text called "the elephants in the room". The book has drawn on observations and analyses of media, popular culture, and the lived experiences of individuals to unpack the power relations, practices and vehicles of governance that have to date rendered these issues all but invisible. Much of it is controversial and, I hope, provocative, but I have endeavoured to locate my arguments robustly where possible within the broader literature and scholarly research. Nevertheless, I acknowledge that pointing out the elephants doesn't automatically make them disappear, nor does it provide a strategy for doing so. It is hoped that these musings will provide the impetus for further research, but also for political action. Sometimes we need to move forward quickly without quite having the evidence base in hand. Historically, political action has often occurred absent such evidence – the Suffragettes had nothing but their own lived experience to help forge their campaign, as did Rosa Parks. How many individuals have to complain about being tired of discrimination before political action can occur? We only need a few to take us seriously in order for a quiet revolution to begin. With that in mind, the following highlights an agenda for change based on two main themes drawn from the foregoing analyses.

Two things

Romantic love is back in fashion after a short hiatus during the 1970s, when it was briefly replaced by sexual promiscuity. Today, romantic love and promiscuity are uneasy bedmates, so to speak. How do we reconcile the Disney/*Twilight* version of romance and enchantment with the expectation of sexual freedom? That is the first thing we have to deal with. The second, and probably more important issue, is how to address the mass frustration felt by half the population at their inability to fulfil their entitlement, their birthright, as Masters of the Universe.[2] I will address this latter issue first.

Up until the 1960s, white men ruled their universe, whether it was a country, a corporation or a household. Their role was as deeply ingrained as their ability to speak or think, and it was unquestionably accepted by Western society as a whole. To their credit, when the civil rights movement took hold and tenaciously refused to release its grip, white men raised the flag and resigned themselves to the inevitability of equal rights. This did not happen overnight of course but it did happen. By the end of the 1970s, women and people of colour were accessing some of the things previously reserved for the privileged group – rights to work, to equal pay and conditions, access to housing and services, and to some measure of respect (Lockyer 2013).

But something happened in the 1980s, and a backlash began to raise its ugly head. By the 1990s, as we saw in Chapter 6, it was in full swing. Faludi (1991) argued that the anti-feminist backlash occurring at that time was more of a pre-emptive strike. Women had not yet achieved equal rights, but there had been several successful campaigns and women's voices were being heard. When the possibility of equal rights loomed, conservatives began to strike back. And while there has been some waxing and waning of this backlash, particularly during times of war, natural disaster and recession, when people were too busy trying to stay alive to worry about such things, the backlash appears to have resumed its path with vigour, most specifically on social media (Moore 2013).

In his research on adolescents' transition into manhood, Michael Kimmel suggests that there are two varieties of backlash – one is clearly misogynistic, the other not so much. The latter variety belongs to the older generation of men, now in their thirties and forties, who, he claims "experience their masculinity wistfully, with nostalgic glances over their shoulders at the carefree boys they once were" (Kimmel 2008: 181):

> As Robert Bly found out a decade ago, when he escorted thousands of men on retreats to retrieve their lost playfulness and innocence, the sober responsibilities of adult masculinity often require men give up their dreams of adventure; daily lives with adult partners and family obligations often mute the ecstatic sexualities of youth.
>
> (Kimmel 2008: 181)

I suggest that the wistfulness experienced by this generation of men also encompasses nostalgia for the dream of being Master of the Universe, taught them by their fathers, but which they eventually became resigned to letting go. The stereotype of the male mid-life crisis in Western society is testament to the social recognition of that resignation. Also, while it is clear that even this generation can be misogynistic, as we saw in the treatment of a female Prime Minister by her political opponents and colleagues alike in Chapter 6, their misogyny does not tend to be spiteful or even intentional – rather, it stems in the main from ignorance and misinformation.

Gen Y men, on the other hand, "experience their masculinity not in terms of what they had to give up in order to become men, but rather they experience it as anticipation – what they *will* experience. And more to the point, what they are *Entitled* to experience" (Kimmel 2008: 181. Emphasis in original).

> And as they begin to bump up against the reality that they're unlikely to be masters of the universe, omnipotent sex gods, and billionaire celebrities hounded by hoardes of groupies, they begin to feel a bit resentful.
>
> (Kimmel 2008: 181)

Brought up with the media literally in their faces 24 hours a day, they have soaked up the promises of advertisers, celebrities and men's magazines of a life in charge and on top of the world. Real life must therefore hit them like a low, hard punch, and they are not taking it lying down. Rather, they are vocalizing their resentment and bitterness on Twitter, Facebook, online forums, and on university campuses, and their anger is aimed at women, gays, and people of colour. Their misogynistic, racist and homophobic diatribes are both spiteful and intentional, and in many cases dangerous. A recent campaign against Twitter for refusing to shut down tweets containing rape threats against women was relatively unsuccessful, and Facebook hosts many sites containing misogynistic and racist content, citing free speech as a rationale (Moore 2013).

The pervasive availability of social media today has made abuse "go viral" and it has exposed vulnerable populations to that abuse in a way that has never before been experienced. Pre-civil rights, the Ku Klux Klan was the only organized group to take vigilante action based on pure hatred and discrimination. Prior to that time, discrimination was experienced more as structural and insidious than as verbal and physical. Today, women are experiencing abuse directly to their faces by individuals and small informal groups, and when someone stands up to protest, they receive rape and death threats.

Simply naming and shaming, or even prosecuting, the offenders does not and will not address the issue. Nor will it prevent rape, child sexual abuse or domestic violence. Public education campaigns and educating women and children about prevention and help-seeking are band-aid solutions that work only for a very small number. The over-riding issue that no one seems to recognize, and that no one therefore has bothered to address, is the way in which media and popular culture govern our beliefs about, and expectations concerning, masculinity, femininity, sex and romantic love. This mish-mash of contradictions and confusions has created a virtual monster. When *Maxim* magazine publishes the 2013 Top 100, what we see is 100 very beautiful, but also very "photoshopped" images of thin, big-breasted, long-legged, symmetrically-featured, successful women. What we fail to realize is that, out of a world population of 7.12 billion, around half of which are presumably women, the existence of 100, 1000 or even 10,000 such women is highly unusual – indeed, they are more than rare, they are almost anomalies. Most of the models appearing in magazines are airbrushed to be thinner, have bigger breasts, shinier hair and flawless skin. Perhaps the 'ideal' of female beauty doesn't even really exist in the flesh. And when we see film after film depicting romantic love as tragic, abusive and inevitable, we forget that these plots and storylines are fabricated, and that the people playing them out are actors (or animated characters). Even "reality" shows are staged. In no sense is *Jersey Shore* a reflection of anyone's real life.

Thus we come back to the first "thing" mentioned above: how to reconcile the Disney/*Twilight* version of romance and enchantment with the expectation of sexual freedom? As we saw in chapters 2 and 3, the popular culture version of romantic love is strongly geared towards fairytale notions of being swept off one's feet, courted and wed, as a prelude to living happily ever after. Film, literature and other cultural depictions reinforce love as fated, inevitable, enduring, exclusive and romantic. People of all ages, but young people especially, are inspired by role models such as UK heir to the throne, Prince William and his wife, Princess Kate, who appear to live in an actual fairytale dream. How quickly the public forgets that William's parents fell afoul of the paradox of romantic love and freedom of sexuality, that his mother was cuckolded by his father, who had a lifelong affair with another man's wife, to whom he is now married; that his mother also had affairs in the end. Her tragic death only reinforced the fairytale – a statue of Princess Diana and her partner, billionaire Dodi Fayed, who died at her side, was erected in Harrod's department store in London in 1998. At the time of writing, the statue still draws hundreds of thousands of visitors every year. Strangely, no one seems to see the irony in celebrating a partnership that was, in fact, the outcome of a broken marriage and an almost-ruined Royal Family. Clearly, Diana had finally found her "true love" in Dodi, and the fact that they died tragically together, many years before their time, just reinforces the fairytale nature of romantic love.

Another example is the ubiquitous celebrity Kim Kardashian, whose marriage to basketball player Kris Humphries, in August 2011, was widely publicized. It was also the subject of a two-part television special featuring the preparation for, and extravagant festivities, which included the launching of Kardashian's "wedding fragrance" in honour of her own wedding. The marriage lasted 72 days, after which Kardashian filed for divorce. Subsequently, it was widely rumoured that the wedding had been a publicity stunt, though Kardashian denied it. She is now engaged to singer Kanye West and has a baby with him called (dare I say it?) North West. At the time of writing, much media attention was being paid to the size of her engagement ring diamond, which apparently is 15 carats, five carats smaller than her previous ring. It would not be overstating to say that the entire Kardashian family is a media circus, with Kim its biggest act. And yet, the public laps up her every move, as she trips from romance to romance, and lawsuit to lawsuit, mesmerized by her fairytale lifestyle. Again, the irony of her personal life seems to have been missed.

If older men are wistful for their masculinity, older women are wistful for romance, and the promise of a life as pampered and adored lover. They will therefore seek it wherever they can, in books, movies, magazines and other media, regardless of how ridiculous it may appear. At the same time as younger men are anticipating their masculine entitlements, young women are anticipating the fairytale of a Disney-like wedding and happily ever after. But unlike young men, who become resentful when they fail to realise their masculine entitlements, young women seem to become confused when they realize that neither marriage nor motherhood is as fairytale as they were led to believe. So ingrained is the plotline of a woman's life, even 40 years after women's liberation tried to tell them it need not be so, that she finds it very difficult to release. Just as young boys are taught that they are the kings of the castle, young girls are taught that they are all princesses. The pervasiveness of media representations, and parental and educational reinforcement, has made it so. It is no wonder that they confuse abuse with the normal characteristics of romantic love.

Sex, love and abuse

The nexus between sex, love and abuse thus resides in the social discourses surrounding masculinity and femininity. While it has always been the case that individuals are governed by the discourses of their time, particularly with respect to masculinity and femininity, today these discourses have an even deeper impact because they are all the more pervasive. Technology ensures not only that we are constantly reminded of the roles we are expected to play, it tells us that it is what we, in fact, want. Our interaction with technology through social media, the internet, gaming and mobile devices allows us to reinforce each other in these roles, and acts as a form of masculinity and femininity policing. It also encourages us to interact with capitalism more than ever before. In an era when poverty is at an all-time high in the Western world, even the poorest have a mobile phone and access to the internet. We are literally being trained to consume almost every moment of every day of our waking lives. I am not suggesting that we are dupes, passively and unconsciously sucking up the roles we are given (Lumby 1997). I am suggesting, however, that it is often difficult to recognize just how pervasive these discourses are and to resist conforming in a world where conforming is rewarded handsomely.

Women's training in femininity and men's training in masculinity do little to prepare them for the realities of sex, love, relationships and children. The subjectivities to which both men and women have access often narrowly define their roles in these contexts. Women must always be cast as victims and men as perpetrators, even in situations where a woman clearly acts against the norm. However, even as they are cast as victims, society fails to give women the tools with which to extract themselves from abusive situations. Instead, they are taught to persevere and to stay quiet and invisible. Men, on the other hand, have no access to victimhood, whether it be sexual, verbal or emotional abuse. Instead, they are taught to "man up", to take control and turn it to their advantage. Thus the 14-year-old boy who is seduced by his 30-year-old female teacher receives pats on the back and high fives from his mates, while the 14-year-old girl who seduces her 30-year-old teacher is cast as the victim because he should have known better.

The rules of masculinity and femininity also spell out quite clearly what each person's role is in a heterosexual relationship. Men must look out for and support their female partners, but not at the expense of their homosocial alliances. The bro code's number one rule is "bros before hoes". And if he doesn't receive his due, then he has cause for complaint. Similarly, women must be coy and sexy, attractive at all times, fashionable and ready for sex. It is her job to maintain the relationship, because everyone knows that men are totally oblivious. Thus, when a woman is emotionally abused by her husband, she looks inward for faults in her words or behaviour, and strives to do better. When she is verbally or physically abused, she becomes frightened, but when he apologizes, as he almost always will, she forgives him because maintaining the relationship is her main goal in life, even over her own physical and mental safety.

Of course, none of this is as simple as it sounds. There are men and women who deliberately and consciously stand outside the parameters of traditional masculinity and femininity. This book is not for them. It is for those who are confused, resentful, wistful or curious about the roles of men and women in heteronormative sex, love and relationships. Domestic abuse is experienced by same-sex couples, people in relationships with transgender individuals and by men at the hands of women and other men. It may also be impacted by race and class, and while I have at points in the book identified these as issues, they are not its focus. Similarly, sexual assault, harassment and abuse is experienced by all genders and sexualities, and by all races and classes. More research on these issues desperately needs to be done, but is also beyond the current book's parameters. Meanwhile, it is hoped that the foregoing chapters do provide a stimulus for further research and discussion, but also a call to political action. The lived experiences of abused women everywhere need to be heard, and loudly enough to drown out the powerful, tenacious and over-whelming chant of the Masters of the Universe. To paraphrase Dylan Thomas, we will "not go gentle into that good night, but rage, rage against the dying of the light".[3]

Notes

2 Enchantment and Romance

1. Written by David Hodges. Copyright *Emi Blackwood Music Inc., Tsbd Louisiana Llc, 1206 Publishing, Summit Base Camp Film Music*. Lyrics from www.eLyrics.net
2. The Twilight Saga (Film Series): Twilight 2008; The Twilight Saga (New Moon) 2009; The Twilight Saga (Eclipse) 2010; The Twilight Saga (Breaking Dawn) Part 1 – 2011, Part 2 – 2012. Developed by Paramount Pictures and based on the novels by Stephanie Myers. Published by Little, Brown and Co.
3. www.wikihow.com/Make-Someone-Fall-in-Love-with-You (Accessed April 23, 2013).
4. www.loveblab.com/make-someone-fall-in-love-with-you (Accessed April 23, 2013).
5. http://wickedsago.blogspot.com.au/2010/02/5-ways-to-make-someone-fall-in-love.html (Accessed April 24, 2013).
6. www.squidoo.com/make-him-love-me (Accessed April 24, 2013).
7. http://attractwomenbooks.com/how-to-attract-women/ (Accessed April 24, 2013).
8. www.examiner.com/article/don-t-put-your-love-life-on-hold-advice-for-single-lesbians-and-lesbian-couples (Accessed April 24, 2013).
9. www.dailystrength.org/c/Lesbian_Relationship_Challenges/advice/16178 514-help-im-love (Accessed April 24, 2013).
10. http://thegaylovecoach.com/category/advice/ (Accessed January 22, 2014).
11. http://thegaylovecoach.com/category/singles-dating/flirting-social-skills/ (Accessed April 24, 2013).
12. www.essentialbaby.com.au/baby (Accessed April 24, 2013).
13. www.huggies.com.au (Accessed April 24, 2013).
14. *Mulan* (1998), *Pocahontas* (1995) and *The Frog Princess* (2009), all produced and distributed by The Walt Disney Company.
15. *Brave* (2012), produced and distributed by The Walt Disney Company.

3 From Disney to Distortion

1. Much of the research for this chapter, especially on the Disney princesses, was conducted by Stephanie Jones. I am very grateful to Stephanie for the many hours of fruitful discussion over the past couple of years on this and other related topics, and for the research projects I have supervised which have contributed to the development of this book.

4   From Distortion to Abuse

1. Mathers, Marshall, Grant, Alexander and Hafermann, Holly (2010) *Love The Way You Lie*. Ferndale, MI: Effigy Studios and Temple Bar, Dublin: Sun Studios.
2. Pink, Basker, Jeff and Ruess, Nate (2013) "Just Give Me a Reason", RCA.

5   Sexual Spaces

1. www.everydaysexism.com. This project is discussed in more detail in Chapter 6.
2. www.womenshealthmag.com/sex-and-relationships (Accessed April 24, 2013).

6   Sexism and Misogyny

1. Available on Youtube at: www.youtube.com/watch?v=SOPsxpMzYw4
2. Available at: www.youtube.com/watch?v=biym0whZK4A
3. Available at: www.youtube.com/watch?v=MnIJxcqSKgY
4. Mosley, Timothy, Hills, Floyd Nathaniel, Jackson, Curtis and Timberlake, Justin R. (2007) *AYO Technology*, Warner/Chappell Music, Inc., Universal Music Publishing Group.
5. MILF is the acronym for "Mother I would love to fuck"; aka a "yummy mummy".
6. Available online at: www.youtube.com/watch?v=4S6qVg0eGgU (Accessed January 22, 2014).
7. Chelley and Ricardo Johnson (2009) *I Took the Night*. Ego/Vae Victis Srl under exclusive licence from Ultra Records, Inc.
8. Sebert, Kesha, Coleman, Joshua and Sebert, Pebe (2010) *Your Love Is My Drug*. Copyright: Sony/ATV Songs LLC, Kecse Rose Music.
9. The series comprises a trilogy authored by E. L. James: *Fifty Shades of Grey*, *Fifty Shades Darker*, and *Fifty Shades Freed* (Vintage Publications Reprint Editions, all 2012).
10. I am grateful to Olivia Hayes for pointing this out.

8   Conclusion – A Geography of Abuse

1. Produced by Button Poetry, 2012. www.youtube.com/watch?v=NW4VvIhhCIM
2. This phrase is borrowed from Kimmel (2008), but was originally coined by Tom Wolff in *Bonfire of the Vanities*, 2008, Picador.
3. Dylan Thomas (1951) "Do Not Go Gentle into That Good Night", originally published in the journal *Botteghe Oscure*.

References

About-face.org (2012) LG Kompressor Plus: Is it Funny to Vacuum Someone's Fat Away? January 29, 2012. Available at: www.about-face.org/lg-kompressor-plus-is-it-funny-to-vacuum-someones-fat-away/ (Accessed January 22, 2014).

Allen, J. (1990) *Sex and Secrets: Crimes Involving Australian Women Since 1880*. Melbourne: Oxford University Press.

Andersen, Hans Christian (1837) *The Little Mermaid*. The Open Library Online. Available at: http://www.openlibrary.org (Accessed February 26, 2014).

Anderson, Eric (2011) *Inclusive Masculinity: The Changing Nature of Masculinities*. Oxon: Routledge.

Anderson, M.A., Gillig, P.M., Sitaker, M., McClosky, K., Malloy, K., and Grigsby, N. (2003) "Why Doesn't She Just Leave?" A Descriptive Study of Victim Reported Impediments to Her Safety. *Journal of Family Violence*, Vol.18, pp. 151–155.

Angel, M.J. (2013) Try this Shopping Nightmare on for Size. *The Sydney Morning Herald*, 7 October 2013. Available at http://www.smh.com.au/lifestyle/fashion/try-this-shopping-nightmare-on-for-size-20131007-2v347.html

Angelides, Steven (2007) Subjectivity under Erasure: Adolescent Sexuality, Gender, and Teacher-Student Sex. *Journal of Men's Studies*, Vol.15, No.3, pp. 347–360.

Aries, Phillipe (1973) *Centuries of Childhood*. Harmondsworth: Penguin.

Aries, Phillipe (1989) From Immodesty to Innocence. In Henry Jenkins (Ed.) *The Children's Culture Reader*. New York: New York University Press. pp.100–103.

Aron, Arthur, Fisher, Greg and Strong, Helen E. (2007) Romantic Love. In Baumeister, Roy F. and Vohs, Katherine D. (eds) *Encyclopedia of Social Psychology*. Los Angeles, CA: Sage Publications p.765.

Australian Government (2009) *Government Response: Inquiry into the Sexualisation of Children in the Contemporary Media Environment*. Available at: http://www.archive.dbcde.gov.au/__data/assets/pdf_file/0003/118182/Inquiry_into_the_sexualisation_of_children_in_the_media.pdf (Accessed February 25, 2014).

Ball, Matthew and Hayes, Sharon (2011) Same-Sex Intimate Partner Violence: Exploring the Parameters. In Burkhard Scherer (Ed.) *Queering Paradigms*. New York: Peter Lang, pp. 161–177.

Bandura, Albert (1971) *Social Learning Theory*. New York: General Learning Press.

Barker, Meg (2012) *Rewriting the Rules: An Integrative Guide to Love, Sex and Relationships*. Oxford: Routledge.

Barker, Meg (2013) Consent is a Grey Area? A Comparison of Understandings of Consent in *Fifty Shades of Grey* and on the BDSM Blogosphere. *Sexualities*, Vol.16, pp. 896–914.

Bates, Laura (2013) Freshers' Week Sexism, and the Damage It Does. *The Guardian*, Friday September 20, 2013. Available at: http://www.theguardian.com/lifeandstyle/the-womens-blog-with-jane-martinson/2013/sep/19/freshers-week-sexism-women (Accessed February 25, 2014).

Bauman, Zigmunt (2003) *Liquid Love: On the Frailty of Human Bonds.* Cambridge: Polity Press.

Bauman, Zigmunt (2004) *Liquid Love: On the Frailty of Human Bonds.* Cambridge: Polity (Kindle Edition).

Bauman, Zigmunt (2008) *The Art of Life.* Cambridge: Polity.

Bauman, Zigmunt and Donskis, Leonidas (2013) *Moral Blindness: The Loss of Sensitivity in Liquid Modernity.* Cambridge: Polity.

Berg, Barbara J. (2009) *Sexism in America: Alive, Well, and Ruining Our Future.* Chicago, IL: Chicago Review Press.

Berlant, Lauren (2007) Slow Death (Sovereignty, Obesity, Lateral Agency). *Critical Inquiry*, Vol.33, No.4, pp. 754–780.

Berlant, Lauren, (2011) *Cruel Optimism.* Durham: Duke University Press.

Beyond Blue (no date) *What Vauses Depression?* Available at: http://www.beyondblue.org.au/the-facts/depression/what-causes-depression (Accessed February 25, 2014).

Branden, Nathaniel (2008) *The Psychology of Romantic Love: Romantic Love in an Anti-romantic Age.* New York: Penguin Group.

Braveheart Inc (2009) Research Documents: Factos and Stats. Available at: www.bravehearts.org.au/docs/facts_and_stats.pdf

Brown, J. (2011) Shame and Domestic Violence: Treatment Perspective for Perpetrators from Self Psychology and Affect Theory. *Sexual and Relationship Therapy*, Vol.19, pp. 39–56.

Brummelman, Eddie, Thomaes, Sander, Slagt, Meike, Overbeek, Geertjan, de Castro, Bram Orobio and Bushman, Brad J. (2013) My Child Redeems My Broken Dreams: On Parents Transferring Their Unfulfilled Ambitions onto Their Child. *Plos One.* Available at: www.plosone.org/article/info%3Adoi%2F10.1371%2Fjournal.pone.0065360 (Accessed February 26, 2014).

Bryan, Jenifer (2012) *From the Dress-Up Corner to the Senior Prom: Navigating Gender and Sexuality Diversity in PreK-12 Schools.* Lanham, MD: Bowman and Littlefield Education.

Burns, Angie (2000) Looking for Love in Intimate Heterosexual Relationships. *Feminism and Psychology*, Vol.10, No.4, pp. 481–485.

Butler, Judith (1990) *Gender Trouble: Feminism and the Subversion of Identity.* New York: Routledge.

Care Notes (2013) "Puberty in boys." *CareNotes.* Truven Health Analytics Inc., 2013. *Health Reference Center Academic.* Available at: http://go.galegroup.com/ps/i.do?id=GALE%7CA347295035&v=2.1&u=qut&it=r&p=HRCA&sw=w&asid=92adefffc9edf5f0642eb23a24f48c0e (Accessed December 20, 2013).

Carr, J.L. and Van Deusen, K.M. (2004) Risk Factors For Male Sexual Aggression on College Campuses. *Journal of Family Violence*, Vol.19, No.5, pp. 279–289.

Carrington, Kerry and Pereira, Margaret A. (2009) *Offending Youth: Crime, Sex and Justice*. Sydney: Federation Press.

Chambers, Deborah (2001) *Representing the Family*. London: Sage.

Chung, D., O'Leary, P.J., and Hand, T. (2006) *Sexual Violence Offenders: Prevention and Intervention Approaches*. ACSSA Issues, No.5. June 2006. Melbourne: Australian Institute for Family Studies.

Claxton, Guy (1997) *Hare Brain, Tortoise Mind: Why Intelligence Increases When You Think Less*. New York: Harper Perennial.

Clulow, Christopher F. (1993) *Rethinking Marriage: Public and Private Perspectives*. London: Tavistock Institute of Medical Psychology.

Commonwealth of Australia (no date) *Voluntary Industry Code of Conduct on Body Image*. Available at: http://www.youth.gov.au/sites/Youth/bodyImage/codeofconduct (Accessed February 25, 2014).

Connell, R.W. (2005) *Masculinities*. Berkeley, CA: University of California Press.

Coontz, Stephanie (2005) *Marriage, A History: From Obedience to Intimacy or How Love Conquered Marriage*. New York: Viking.

Coppinger, Robert M. and Rosenblatt, Paul C. (1968) Romantic Love and Subsistence Dependence of Spouses. *Southwestern Journal of Anthropology* Vol. 24, No.3, pp. 310–319.

Cornish, Lisa (2013) *Aussies Spend Up Big to Ensure Their Kids have it All: Kidspot*, Available at: http://parenting.kidspot.com.au/aussies-spend-up-big-to-ensure-their-kids-have-it-all/#.UrDreo2RPZs (Accessed February 26, 2014).

Cortoni, F. and Gannon, T. (2011) "Introduction" to Special Issue on Female Sexual Offenders. *Journal of Sexual Aggression*, Vol.17, No.1, pp. 1–3.

Cott, Nancy (2000) *Public Vows: A History of Marriage and the Nation*. Cambridge, MA: Harvard University Press.

Crime and Misconduct Commission. (2005) *Policing Domestic Violence in Queensland*. Brisbane: Crime and Misconduct Commission.

Davidson, Julia C. (2008) *Child Sexual Abuse: Media Representations and Government Reactions*. Abingdon, UK: Routledge-Cavendish.

Davis, Geena (2004) Geena Davis Institute on Gender and Media. Available at: http://www.thegeenadavisinstitute.org/index.php (Accessed February 25, 2014).

De Botton, Alain (1997) *How Proust Can Change Your Life*. London: Picador.

De Botton, Alain (1998) *How Proust Can Change Your Life*. Vintage Press.

De Botton, Alain (2006) *The Architecture of Happiness*. New York: Pantheon

De Botton, Alain (2012) *How to Think More About Sex*. London: Picador.

Deering, R. and Mellor, D. (2011) An Exploratory Qualitative Study of the Self-Reported Impact of Female-Perpetrated Childhood Sexual Abuse. *Journal of Child Sexual Abuse*, Vol.20, No.1, pp. 58–76.

Dehaas, Josh (2013) McGill Students Won't Ban Blurred Lines. *McLeans Online*. October 31, 2013. Available at: http://oncampus.macleans.ca/education/tag/sexual-assault/

Denov, M. S. (2004) *Perspectives on Female Sex Offending*. Surrey: Ashgate Publishing.

Denov, M.S. (2003) The Myth of Innocence: Sexual Scripts and the Recognition of Child Sexual Abuse by Female Perpetrators. *The Journal of Sex Research*, Vol. 40, No.3, pp. 303–314.

Denzin, Norman K. (1997) *Interpretive Ethnography*. Thousand Oaks, CA: Sage.

Dines, Gail (2010) *Pornland: How Porn Has Hijacked Our Sexuality*. Boston, MA: Beacon Press (Kindle Edition).

Disney Media (no date) *Princess*. Available at: http://www.disneymediaplus.co.uk/content/princess audiences (Accessed February 25, 2014).

Disney/Pixar (no date) *Disney Princesses*. Available at: http://www.home.disney.com.au/disneyfilms/princess.html (Accessed February 25, 2014).

Donovan, C., and Hester, M. (2010) "I Hate the Word 'victim'": An Exploration of Recognition of Domestic Violence in Same Sex Relationships. *Social Policy and Society*, Vol.9, pp. 279–289.

Douglas, H., and Stark, T. (2010) *Stories from Survivors: Domestic Violence and Criminal Justice Interventions*. Brisbane: University of Queensland.

Douglas, Susan J. (2010) *The Rise of Enlightened Sexism: How Pop Culture Took Us from Girl Power to Girls Gone Wild*. New York: St. Martin's Griffin.

Driscoll, C. (2002) *Girls: Feminine Adolescence in Popular Culture and Cultural Theory*. New York: Columbia University Press.

Dutton, D.G., and Corvo, K. (2006) Transforming a Flawed Policy: A Call to Revive Psychology and Science in Domestic Violence Research and Practice. *Aggression and Violent Behavior*, Vol.11, pp. 457–483.

Dymock, Alex (2013) Flogging Sexual Transgression: Interrogating the Costs of the "*Fifty Shades* effect". *Sexualities*, Vol.16, pp. 880–895.

Eastwood, C. (2003) The Experiences of Child Complainants of Sexual Abuse in the Criminal Justice System. *Trends and issues in Crime and Criminal Justice*. May 2003.

Egan, R. Danielle (2013) *Becoming Sexual: A Critical Appraisal of the Sexualisation of Girls*. Cambridge: Polity Press.

Ellingson, Laura. L., and Ellis, Carolyn. (2008) Autoethnography as Constructionist Project. In J. A. Holstein and J. F. Gubrium (Eds.), *Handbook of Constructionist Research*. New York: Guilford Press, pp. 445–466.

Elshof, L. (2003) Technological Education, Interdisciplinarity, and the Journey Toward Sustainable Development: Nurturing New Communities of Practice. *Canadian Journal of Science, Mathematics and Technology Education*, Vol.3, No.4, pp. 165–184.

Epstein, D. (1999) Effective Intervention in Domestic Violence Cases: Rethinking the Roles of Prosecution, Judges and the Court System. *Yale Journal of Law and Feminism*, Vol.11, No.3, pp. 3–50.

Evans, I. (2002) Picturesque Falsehoods: An Examination of Romantic Love, the Press and Domestic Violence. *Outskirts*, Vol.9, pp. 1–17.

Faludi, Susan (1991) *Backlash: The Undeclared War Against American Women*. New York: Crown Publishers.

Faludi, Susan (2000) *Stiffed: The Betrayal of the American Man*. Hammersmith: HarperCollins.

Fauske, J.R., Mullen, C.A. and Sutton, L.C. (2006) Educator Sexual Misconduct in Schools: Implications for leadership preparation. In D.C. Thompson
and F.E. Crampton (Eds.) *Exploring Contested Intersections of Democracy, Social
Justice and Globalization: University Council for Educational Administration
Conference Proceedings for Convention 2006*, San Antonio, TX, pp. 1–16.

Faw, Larissa (2012) Why Millennials Are Spending More Than They Earn,
and Parents Are Footing the Bill. *Forbes*. Available at: www.forbes.com/sites/
larissafaw/2012/05/18/why-millennials-are-spending-more-than-they-earn/

Feinberg, Joel (1985) *The Moral Limits of the Criminal Law. Volume One: Offense
to Others*. New York: Oxford University Press.

Fletcher, Tony (2003) *Hedonism: A Novel*. London: Omnibus Press.

Foley, Sallie, Kope, Sally A., and Sugrue, Dennis P. (2012) *Sex Matters For
Women: A Complete Guide to Taking Care of Your Sexual Self*. Second Edition.
New York, NY: Guilford Press.

Foote, L. (2012) I Want to be a Princess Too: Exploring the Blackout of
Disney's Princesses and Controversies Surrounding The Princess and the
Frog and Its Effects on African American Girls. *Film Matters*, Vol.2, No.3,
pp. 13–22.

Foreman, Sean, Sebert, Kesha and Levin, Benjamin (2010) *Blah, Blah, Blah*.
Copyright: Cagje Music, Dynamite Cop Music, Matza Ball Music, Emi
Blackwood Music Inc., Master Falcon Music.

Foucault, M. (1982) The Subject and Power. In J. Faubion (Ed.). *Power: Essential
Works of Foucault 1954–1984, Volume 3*. London: Penguin Books.

Foucault, M. (1995) *Discipline and Punish: The Birth of the Prison*. New York:
Vintage Books.

Foucault, M. (1998) *The Will to Knowledge: The History of Sexuality Volume 1*.
London: Penguin.

Frankel, Carl (2010) Kinky Sex: When Did BDSM Become So Wildly Popular?
Alternet. June 2, 2010. Available at: www.alternet.org/story/147084/kinky_
sex%3A_when_did_bdsm_become_so_wildly_popular (Accessed October
29, 2013).

Fraser, H. (2005) Women, Love, and Intimacy "gone wrong": Fire, Wind and
Ice. *Affilia*, Vol.20, pp. 10–20.

Freeman, N.J. and Sandler, J.C. (2008) Female and Male Sex Offenders: A Comparison of Recidivism Patterns and Risk Factors. *Journal of Interpersonal
Violence*, Vol.23, No.10, pp. 1394–1413.

Fuselier, D., Durham, R. and Wurtele, S. (2002) The Child Sexual Abuser:
Perceptions of College Students and Professionals. *Sexual Abuse: A Journal
of Research and Treatment*, Vol.14, No.3, pp. 271–280.

Gakhal, B. and Brown, S. (2011) A Comparison of the General Public's, Foren-
sic Professionals' and Students' Attitudes Towards Female Sex Offenders.
Journal of Sexual Aggression, Vol.17, No.1, pp. 105–116.

Gavin, H. (2005) The Social Construction of the Child Sex Offender Explored
by Narrative. *The Qualitative Report*, Vol.10, pp. 395–415.

Giorgio, G. (2002) Speaking Silence: Definitional Dialogues in Abusive Lesbian
Relationships. *Violence Against Women*, Vol.8, pp. 1233–1259.

Gleb, Karen (2007) *Recidivism of Sex Offenders: A Research Paper*. Melbourne: Sentencing Advisory Council, Victoria. Available at: www.deakin.edu.au/ hmnbs/psychology/pdf-docs/colloquia/reading-for-1-aug-graffam2.pdf.

Goldie, P. (2007) There Are Reasons and Reasons. In D. Hutto and M. Ratcliffe (Eds.) *Folk Psychology Re-Assessed*. Dordrecht: Springer, pp. 103–114.

Goldsworthy, Anna (2013) Unfinished Business: Sex, Freedom and Misogyny. *Quarterly Essay Series*. No.50.

Graham, Linda J. (2005) Discourse Analysis and the Critical use of Foucault. Paper presented to the *Australian Association for Research in Education 2005 Annual Conference*, Sydney, 27 November–1 December, 2005.

Halberstam, Jack (2013) *Gaga Feminism: Sex, Gender and the End of Normal*. Boston, MA: Beacon Press.

Hayes, Sharon and Carpenter, Belinda (2012) Social Moralities and Discursive Constructions of Female Sex Offenders. *Sexualities*, Vol.16, No.1–2, pp. 147–157.

Hayes, Sharon and Jeffries, Samantha (2013) Why Do They Keep Going Back? Exploring Women's Discursive Experiences of Intimate Partner Abuse. *International Journal of Criminology and Sociology*, Vol.1, No.2, pp. 57–71.

Hayes, Sharon, Carpenter, Belinda and Dwyer, Angela (2012) *Sex, Crime and Morality*. London: Routledge.

Henneberg, Maceij (2002) 2002 National Size and Shape Survey. Available at http://www.researchgate.net/publication/233726506_2003_National_size_ and_shape_survey

Herbert, T.B., Silver, R.C., and Ellard, J. (1991) Coping with an Abusive Relationship: How and Why Do Women Stay? *Journal of Marriage and the Family*, Vol.53, pp. 311–325.

Hite, Shere (2003) *The Hite Report: A Nationawide Study of Female Sexuality*. New York, NY: Seven Stories Press.

Hite, Shere (2008) Female Orgasm Today: The Hite Report's Research Then and Now. *On The Issues: A Magazine of Feminist, Progressive Thinking* (Summer 2008). Available at: www.ontheissuesmagazine.com/july08/july2008_6.php

Hodges, David (2011) *A Thousand Years*. Copyright Emi Blackwood Music Inc., Tsbd Louisiana Llc, 1206 Publishing, Summit Base Camp Film Music.

Hotten, J. (2009) *The "utopian nightmare": Key Issues about Lesbian Domestic Violence According to Brisbane Domestic Violence Services*. (unpublished Honours dissertation). Brisbane: Queensland University of Technology.

Huffington Post, The (2012) Anal Sex More Popular Than Possibly Expected Among Heterosexual Couples: Center for Disease Control and Prevention Report. *The Huffington Post* (author not stated), January 6, 2012. Available at: www.huffingtonpost.com/2012/01/06/anal-sex-heterosexual-couples-report_n_1190440.html (Accessed October 29, 2013).

Hunter, R. (2006) Narratives of Domestic Violence. *Sydney Law Review*, Vol.28, pp. 733–776.

Illouz, Eva (1997) *Consuming the Romantic Utopia: Love and the Cultural Contradictions of Capitalism*. Berkley: University of California Press.

IMDB (1998) *Snow White and the Seven Dwarves.* Available at: http://www. imdb.com/title/tt0029583 (Accessed February 25, 2014).

IMDB (no date) Quotes from *Magnolia.* Available at: http://www.imdb.com/ title/tt0175880/quotes (Accessed February 25, 2014).

Ingraham, Chrys (2008) *White Weddings: Romancing Heterosexuality in Popular Culture.* New York: Routledge, Second Edition.

Jackson, Stevi (1993) Even Sociologists Fall in Love: An Exploration in the Sociology of Emotions. *Sociology,* Vol.27, No.2, pp. 201–220.

Jankowiak, William R. and Fischer, Edward F. (1992) A Cross Cultural Perspective on Romantic Love. *Ethnology,* Vol.31, No.2, pp. 149–155.

Johnson, H., Ollus, N., and Nevala, S. (2007) *Violence against Women: An International Perspective.* London: Springer.

Johnson, Merri Lisa (2002) Fuck You and Your Untouchable Face: Third Wave Feminism and the Problem of Romance. In Merri Lisa Johnson (Ed.) *Jane Sexes It Up: True Confessions of Feminist Desire.* New York/London: Four Walls Eight Windows.

Johnson, R., Gilchrist, E., Beech, A.R., Weston, S., Takriti, R., and Freeman, R. (2006) The Psychometric Typology of U.K. Domestic Violence Offenders. *Journal of Interpersonal Violence,* Vol.21, pp. 1270–1285.

Jones, Gemma (2012) Prime Minister Julia Gillard Trades Blows with Abbott Over Sexism, Misogyny, Peter Slipper and Claims about her Father. *The Australian.* October 9, 2012. Available at: www.theaustralian. com.au/news/prime-minister-julia-gillard-trades-blows-with-abbott-over-sexism-misogyny-peter-slipper-and-claims-about-her-father/story-e6frg 6n6-1226492391473 (Accessed December 18, 2013).

Jong, Erica (2011) *Fear of Flying.* Iconic Ebooks/Open Road Media (Kindle Edition).

Karan, A., and Keating, L. (2007) The Precursor to Domestic Violence. *Judges' Journal,* Summer, pp. 23–28.

Kaye, Kerwin (2005). Sexual Abuse Victims and the Wholesome Family: Feminist, Psychological and State Discourses. In Elizabeth Bernstein and Laurrie Schaffer (Eds.) *Regulating Sex: The Politics of Intimacy and Identity.* New York: Routledge.

Keith, Thomas (2012) *The Bro Code: How Contemproary Culture Creates Sexist Men.* New Media Foundation. Available at: www.mediaed.org/cgi-bin/ commerce.cgi?preadd=action&key=246

Keller, Timothy and Keller, Kathy (2013) *The Meaning of Marriage.* New York, NY: Riverhead Trade.

Kellogg, Nancy D. (2010) Sexual Behaviors in Children: Evaluation and Management. *American Family Physician,* Vol.82, No.10, pp. 1233–1238.

Kilbourne, J., and Levin, D.E. (2008) *So Sexy so Soon : The New Sexualized Childhood, and What Parents Can Do To Protect Their Kids.* New York: Ballantine Books.

Kimmel, Michael S. (2005) *The Gender of Desire: Essays on Male Sexuality.* New York, NY: SUNY Press.

Kimmel, Michael S. (2008) *Guyland: The Perilous World Where Boys Become Men.* New York: Harper Perennial.

Kingston, Ann (2013) The Real Danger for Women on Campus. *McLeans Online*. November 27, 2013. Available at: http://oncampus.macleans.ca/education/tag/sexual-assault/

Klotman, Phyllis R. (1979) Dick-and-Jane and the Shirley Temple Sensibility in "The Bluest Eye". *Black American Literature Forum*, Vol.13, No.4, pp.123–125.

Knesz, Greulich (2007) *How Young People Learn About Gender: The Influence of Parents and Peers*. Doctoral Dissertation. New York: New York University.

Kokkola, Lydia (2011) Virtuous Vampire and Voluptuous Vamps: Romance Conventions reconsidered in Stephanie Meyer's "Twilight" Series. *Children's Literature in Education*, Vol.42, pp. 165–179.

Landor, Roland V. (2009) Double Standards? Representation of Male vs Female Sex offenders in the Australian Media. *Griffith Working Papers in Pragmatics and Intercultural Communication*, Vol.2, No.2, pp. 84–93.

Leahy, Michael (2008) *Porn Nation: Conquering America's #1 Addiction*. Chicago: Northfield Publishing.

Leonard, W., A., Mitchell, M., Pitts., S., and Patel, S. (2008) *Coming Forward: The Underreporting of Heterosexist Violence and Same Sex Partner Abuse in Victoria*. Melbourne: Victoria Law Foundation.

Lewis, Reina and Mills, Sara (Eds.) (2003) *Feminist Post Colonial Theory: A Reader*. New York: Routledge.

Lockyer, Bridget (2013) An Irregular Period? Participation in the Bradford Women's Liberation Movement: Women's History Review. *Special Issue: 20 Years of the Women's History Network (UK): Looking Back – Looking Forward*, Vol.22, No.4, pp. 543–657.

Lovett, Edward (2012) Most Models Meet Criteria for Anorexia, Size 6 is a Plus Size: Magazine. ABC News January 12, 2012. Available at http://abcnews.go.com/blogs/headlines/2012/01/most-models-meet-criteria-for-anorexia-size-6-is-plus-size-magazine/ (Accessed January 22, 2014).

Lowen, Alexander (2004) *Narcissism: Denial of the True Self*. Camaray, NSW: Simon and Schuster.

Lumby, Catharine and Albury, Kath (2010) Too Much? Too Young? The Sexualisation of Children Debate in Australia. *Media International Australia*. No. 135, pp. 141–152.

Lumby, Catherine (1997) *Bad Girls: The Media, Sex and Feminism*. Melbourne: Allen and Unwin.

Lyons, Christopher J. (2008) Individual Perceptions and the Social Construction of Hate Crimes: A Factorial Survey. *The Social Science Journal*, Vol. 45, No.1, pp. 107–131.

Lystra, Karen (1989) *Searching the Heart: Women, Men, and Romantic Love in Nineteenth-Century America*. New York: Oxford University Press.

Mason, G. (1997) Boundaries of Sexuality: Lesbian Experiences of Feminist Discourse on Violence against Women. *Australian Gay and Lesbian Law Journal*, Vol.7, pp. 41–59.

Maxim (2003) How to Cure a Feminist. *Maxim Magazine*. November 2003 Issue.

McCann, Carole R. and Kim, Seung Kyung (Eds.) (2010) *Feminist Theory: A Reader*. Second Edition. London: Routledge.

McClelland, S.I. and Fine, M. (2008) Writing on Cellophane: Studying Teen Women's Sexual Desires; Inventing Methodological Release Points. In K. Gallagher (Ed.), *The Methodological Dilemma: Creative, Critical and Collaborative Approaches to Qualitative Research.* London: Routledge, pp. 232–260.

Media Education Foundation (2011) *The Bro Code* transcript. Available at http://www.mediaed.org/assets/products/246/transcript_246.pdf (Accessed February 26, 2014).

Merrill, G.S. (1996) Theoretical Perspectives – Ruling the Exceptions: Same-Sex Battering and Domestic Violence Theory. In C.M. Renzitti and C.H. Miley (Eds.) *Violence in Gay and Lesbian Domestic Partnerships.* Binghamton: Harrington Park Press.

Merrish, Lori (1996) Cuteness and Commodity Aesthetics: Tom Thumb and Shirley Temple. In Thompson, Rosemary Garland (Ed.) *Freakery: Cultural Spectacles of the Extraordinary Body.* New York: New York University Press.

Mersch, John (no date) Tween: Child Development (9–11 Years). *Medicine.net.* Available at: www.medicinenet.com/tween_child_development/article.htm (Accessed February 26 2014).

Moore, Suzanne (2013) The Backlash Against Feminism Aims to Preserve the "Manosphere". *The Guardian,* Thursday August 2, 2013.

Moran, J. (2002) *Interdisciplinarity.* London: Routledge.

Morison, S. and Greene, E. (1992) Juror and Expert Knowledge of Child Sexual Abuse. *Child Abuse and Neglect,* 16, 595–613.

Morrish, Liz and Sauntson, Helen (2007) *New Perspectives on Language and Sexual Identity.* Houndmills: Palgrave Macmillan.

Mouzos, J., and Makkai, T. (2004) *Women's Experiences of Male Violence: Findings from the Australian Component of the International Violence Against Women Survey.* Canberra: Australian Institute of Criminology.

Mugford, J. (1989) *National Committee on Violence: Domestic Violence.* Canberra: Australian Institute of Criminology.

Mullins, Andrew (2000) Average Dress Size of Women Increases to 14. *The Independent,* 26 June 2000. Available at http://www.independent.co.uk/news/uk/this-britain/average-dress-size-of-women-increases-to-14-715277.html

Myers, Lily (2013) Shrinking Women. *Button Poetry.* Available at https://www.youtube.com/watch?v=zQucWXWXp3k

Nathan, Pamela and Ward, Tony (2002) Female Child Sex Offenders: Clinical and Demographic Features. *Journal of Sexual Aggression,* Vol.8, No.1, pp. 5–21.

Neame, A. and Heenan, M. (2003) *What Lies Behind the Hidden Figure of Sexual Assault? Issues of Prevalence and Disclosure.* Australian Centre for the Study of Sexual Assault Briefing Paper, No 1.

Negy Hesse-Biber, Sharlene (Ed.) (2012) *Handbook of Feminist Research: Theory and Praxis.* Second Edition. London: Sage.

Newman, David and Smith, Rebecca (1999) *The Social Construction of Childhood.* Newbury Park: Pine Forge Press.

Newport, Frank (2012) *God is Alive and Well: The Future of Religion in America.* Washington, DC: Gallup Press.

Niffenegger, Audrey (2004) *The Time Traveller's Wife*. Chicago, IL: Houghton Mifflin Harcourt.

O'Brien, Erin, Hayes, Sharon and Carpenter, Belinda (2013) *The Politics of Sex Trafficking: A Moral Geography*. Oxon: Palgrave Macmillan.

Oakley, Lisa (2004) *Cognitive Development*. New York: Routledge.

Oliver, J. Eric (2006) *Fat Politics: The Real Story Behind America's Obesity Epidemic*. Oxford: Oxford University Press.

Orenstein, Peggy (2011) *Cinderella Ate My Daughter*. New York: HarperCollins.

Overington, Caroline (2013) Liberal Menu on Gillard: "Small Breasts, Big Thighs and a Big Red Box". *The Australian Women's Weekly* online, Wednesday June 12, 2013. Available at: http://aww.ninemsn.com.au/news/newsstories/8673507/liberal-menu-on-gillard-small-breasts-huge-thighs-and-big-red-box (Accessed October 29, 2013).

Person, Ethel Specter (1991) Romantic Love: At the Intersection of the Psyche and the Cultural Unconscious. *Journal of the American Psychoanalytic Association*, Vol.39, No.5, pp. 383–411.

Pitts, M., Smith, A., Mitchell, A., and Patel, S. (2006) *Private Lives: A Report on the Health and Wellbeing of GLBT Australians*. Melbourne: Australian Research Centre in Sex Health and Society.

Power, C., Koch, T., Kralik, D., and Jackson, D. (2006) Lovestruck: Women, Romantic Love and Intimate Partner Violence. *Contemporary Nurse*, Vol.21, No.1, pp. 74–185.

Ptacek, J. (1999) *Battered Women in the Courtroom: The Power of Judicial Responses*. Boston: Northeastern University Press.

Queensland Government (no date) *What is Child Abuse?* Available at: http://www.communities.qld.gov.au/childsafety/protecting-children/what-is-child-abuse (Accessed February 25, 2014).

Radwan, M. Farouk (2008) *How to Make Someone Fall in Love With You: Based on the Psychology of Falling in Love*. 2knowmyself.com

Renold, Emma and Ringrose, Jessica (2011) Schizoid subjectivities? Re-theorizing teen girls' sexual cultures in an era of 'sexualization'. *Journal of Sociology*. Vol. 47, No. 4, 389–409.

Renzetti, Claire M. (1992) *Violent Betrayal: Partner Abuse in Lesbian Relationships*. Thousand Oaks, CA: Sage Publications.

Renzetti, Claire M. (2009) Intimate Partner Violence and Economic Disadvantage. In Evan Stark and Eve Buzawa (Eds.) *Violence Against Women in Families and Relationships: Victimization and Community Response*. Santa Barbara, CA: Praeger/Greenwood, pp. 73–92

Ristock, Janice L. (2002) *No More Secrets: Violence in Lesbian Relationships*. New York, NY: Routledge.

Rosenblatt, Paul C. (1967) Marital Residence and the Functions of Romantic Love. *Ethnology*. Vol.6, No.4, pp. 471–480.

Rossi, P. and Nock, S. (1982) *Measuring Social Judgments: The Factorial Survey Approach*. Beverly Hills: Sage.

Royal College of Psychiatrists (2011) *Mental Health of Students in Higher Education: College Report CR116*. London: Royal College of Psychiatrists.

Rush, Emma and La Nauze, Andrea (2006) *Corporate Paedophilia: Sexualisation of Children in Australia. Discussion Paper Number 90.* Canberra: The Australia Institute.

Russell, V. Michelle and McNulty, James K. (2011) Frequent Sex Protects Intimates From the Negative Implications of Their Neuroticism *Social Psychological and Personality Science* Vol.2, No.2, pp. 220–227.

Salter, Jessica (2008) Women's Dresses are Getting Bigger. *The Telegraph,* 15 September 2008. Available at http://www.telegraph.co.uk/health/2961016/ Womens-dresses-are-getting-bigger.html

Sambrook, S., Stewart, J., and Roberts, C. (2008) Doctoral Supervision: Glimpses from Above, Below and in the Middle. *Journal of Further and Higher Education,* Vol.32, No.1, pp. 71–84.

Saradjian, Jacqui and Hanks, Helga G.I. (2010) *Women Who Sexually Abuse Children: From Research to Clinical Practice.* New York: Wiley.

Schneider, F.W., Gruman, J.A., and Coutts, L.M. (Eds.) (2005) *Applied Social Psychology: Understanding and Addressing Social and Practical Problems.* Thousand Oaks, CA: Sage Publications.

Scully, Diana (1994) *Understanding Sexual Violence: A Study of Convicted Rapists.* New York: Routledge.

Seiter, Ellen (1995) *Sold Separately: Parents and children in Consumer Culture.* New Brunswick, NJ: Rutgers University Press.

Sharp Dummies (2013) Survey Data. Available at http://www.sharpdummies. com.au/survey_data.mhtml

Shaver, Philip R., and Mikulincer, Mario (Eds.) (2012) *Meaning, Mortality and Choice: The Social Psychology of Existential Concerns.* Washington, DC: The American Psychological Association.

Simon, Herbert (1972) Theories of Bounded Rationality, In C.B. McGuire and R. Radner (Eds.) *Decision and Organization.* Amsterdam: North-Holland Publishing Company.

Sioux, Tracee (2011) *Love Distortion: Belle, Battered Co-dependent and Other Love Stories.* Fort Collins: The Girl Revolution LLC (Kindle Edition).

Skinner, B. F. (1953) *Science and Human Behavior.* New York: The Free Press.

Smart, Carol (1992) Disruptive Bodies and Unruly Sex: The Regulation of Reproduction and Sexuality in the Nineteenth Century. In Carol Smart (Ed.) *Regulating Womanhood: Historical Essays on Marriage, Motherhood and Sexuality.* London: Routledge.

Smith, Melinda and Segal, Jeanne (2013) Domestic Violence and Abuse. *The HelpPage,* July 2013. Available at: www.helpguide.org/mental/domestic_ violence_abuse_types_signs_causes_effects.htm (Accessed October 29, 2013).

Smith, Tom W. (1990) A Report: The Sexual Reviolution. *The Public Opinion Quarterly,* Vol.54, No.3 (Autumn), pp. 415–435.

Soble, Eric (1989) *Eros, Agape and Philia: Readings in the Philosophy of Love.* New York: Paragon House.

Strube, M.J., and Barbour, L.S. (1983) The Decision to Leave an Abusive Relationship: Economic Sependence and Psychological Commitment. *Journal of Marriage and the Family,* Vol.45, pp. 785–963.

Styles, Ruth and McCann, Charlie (2013) It's a Cinch! Woman Gets a Miniscule 16 inch Waist by Sleeping in a Corset for THREE years (and she still wants to get smaller). *The Daily Mail*, 19 June 2013. Available at: http://www.dailymail.co.uk/femail/article-2338647/Its-cinch-Woman-gets-miniscule-16-inch-waist-sleeping-corset-THREE-years-wants-smaller.html

Sugarman, David B., and Susan L. Frankel (1996) Patriarchal Ideology and Wife-assault: A Meta-analytic Review. *Journal of Family Violence* Vol.11, No. 1, pp. 13–40.

Taylor, Anthea (2012) "The Urge Toward Love is the Urge Toward Death": Romance, Masochistic Desire and Postfeminism in the *Twilight* Novels. *International Journal of Cultural Studies,* Vol.15, No.1, pp. 31–46.

Taylor, Sandra C. (2004) Researching Educational Policy and Change in 'new times': Using Critical Discourse Analysis. *Journal of Education Policy*, Vol. 19, No. 4, pp. 433–451.

The Australian (2013) Julia Gillard's Clumsy and Manipulative Gender War. *The Australian.* June 13, 2013. Available at: http://www.theaustralian.com.au/opinion/editorials/julia-gillards-clumsy-and-manipulative-gender-war/story-e6frg71x-1226662755252 (Accessed February 25, 2014).

The Canadian Press (2013) Another Sex Attack on UBC Campus. *McLeans Online.* October 29, 2013. Available at: http://oncampus.macleans.ca/education/tag/sexual-assault/

The Independent (2010) Neurotic People Need More Sex (author not stated). Available at: www.independent.co.uk/life-style/health-and-families/neurotic-people-need-more-sex-2154509.html

Thomas, Terry (2005) *Sex Crime: Sex Offending and Society*. Second Edition. London: Willan Publishing.

Titzmann, P. F. (2012) Growing Up Too Soon? Parentification Among Immigrant and Native Youth in Germany. *Journal of Youth and Adolescence*, Vol.41, pp. 880–893.

Townsend, Mark and Syal, Rajeev (2009) Up to 64,000 Women in UK "are child-sex offenders". *The Observer*, Sunday October 4, 2009. Available at: www.guardian.co.uk/society/2009/oct/04/uk-female-child-sex-offenders (Accessed February 26, 2014).

UN Committee on the Rights of the Child (2013) *Ratification of the Convention on the Rights of the Child*, January 2013. Office of the High Commissioner for Human Rights, United Nations. Available at http://www.ohchr.org/EN/HRBodies/CRC/Pages/CRCIndex.aspx.

UNICEF (2005) *The Media and Children's rights*. Available at http://www.communities.qld.gov.au/childsafety/protecting-children/what-is-child-abuse (accessed February 25, 2014).

Vandiver, D.M. and Walker, J.T. (2002) Female Sex Offenders: An Overview and Analysis of 40 cases. *Criminal Justice Review*, Vol.27, pp. 284–300.

Walker, Lenore (1979) *The Battered Woman*. New York: Harper and Row.

Wallach-Scott, Joan (2011) *The Fantasy of Feminist History*. Durham: Duke University Press.

Walter, Natasha (2010) *Living Dolls: The Return of Sexism*. London: Virago.

Wardrop, Murray (2009) Kate Moss: 'Nothing taskes as good as skinny feels'. *The Telegraph*, November 19, 2009. Available at http://www.telegraph. co.uk/news/celebritynews/6602430/Kate-Moss-Nothing-tastes-as-good-as-skinny-feels.html

Warren, Natasha (2013) Geordie Shores: The Big Mac of the Junk TV World. *Sabotage Times*. February 22, 2013. Available at: http://sabotagetimes. com/reportage/geordie-shore-the-big-mac-of-the-junk-tv-world/ (Accessed December 19, 2013).

Warren, Rossalyn (2013) If You Know Someone Who Doesn't Believe in Sexism, Show Them This. *Upworthy*. Available at: www.upworthy.com/ if-you-know-someone-who-doesnt-believe-sexism-exists-show-them-this

Warrington, Vanessa (2013) What Body Shape is Average in Australia? *Readers Digest Online*. Available at: http://www.readersdigest.com.au/what-body-shape-is-average

Weatherall, Margaret (1995) Romantic Discourse and Feminist Analysis: Interrogating Investment, Power and Desire. In Kitzinger, Celia and Wilkinson, Sue (Eds.) *Feminism and Discourse: Psychological Perspectives*. London: Sage.

Weeks, Jeffrey (2007) *The World We Have Won: The Remaking of Erotic and Intimate Life*. Oxford: Routledge.

Wei Luo (2012) Selling Cosmetic Surgery and Beauty Ideals: The Female Body in the Web Sites of Chinese Hospitals. *Women's Studies in Communication*. Vol.35, No.1, pp. 68–95.

Weiderman, Michael W. (2005) The Gendered nature of Sexual Scripts. *The Family Journal: Counselling and Therapy for Couples and Families,* Vol.13, No.4, pp. 496–502.

Weldon, Fay (2012) *Godless in Eden*. Hammersmith: HarperCollins Publishers.

Wetherall, Margaret (1995) Romantic Discourse and Feminist Analysis: Interrogating Investment, Power and Desire. In Celia Kitzinger and Sue Wilkinson (Eds.) *Feminism and Discourse: Psychological Perspectives*. London: Sage.

Wilding, Raelene (2003) Romantic Love and "Getting Married": Narratives of the Wedding In and Out of Cinema Texts. *Journal of Sociology*, Vol.39, No.4, pp. 373–389.

Williams, Zoe (2012) The Saturday Interview: Stuart Hall. *The Guardian*, Saturday February 11, 2012. Available at: www.theguardian.com/theguardian/ 2012/feb/11/saturday-interview-stuart-hall (Accessed October 30, 2013).

Wolf, Naomi (2002) *The Beauty Myth: How Images of Beauty Are Used Against Women*. Reprint Edition. New York: Harper Perennial.

Wood, J.T. (2001) The Normalisation of Violence in Heterosexual Romantic Relationships: Women's Narratives of Love and Violence. *Journal of Social and Personal Relationships*, Vol.18, pp. 239–261.

World of Tales (no date) Available at: http://www.worldoftales.com (Accessed February 25, 2014).

Wurtele, S.K. Kvaternick, M. and Franklin, C.F. (1992) Sexual Abuse Prevention for Preschoolers: A Survey of Parents' Behaviors, Attitudes and Beliefs. *Journal of Child Sexual Abuse*, Vol.1, pp. 113–128.

Index

CPSIA information can be obtained at www.ICGtesting.com
Printed in the USA
LVOW05*0336040215

425578LV00006B/30/P